From Scorn
to Dignity

A Brief History of Disability

Other Titles by Bryan Breed

Non-Fiction

People You Meet
The Man Outside
Famous Mysteries of the Sea
I Know A Rotten Place
White Collar Bird
Off The Record

Fiction

Match (with Mary St. George)
Oh Lord Villy
Going Down On Chelsea Reach

From Scorn to Dignity

A Brief History of Disability

Bryan Breed

NEW EUROPEAN PUBLICATIONS LONDON

Published in the United Kingdom in 2008 by

New European Publications Limited
14-16 Carroun Road
London SW8 1JT, England

British Library Cataloguing in Publication Data

ISBN 978 187 2410 333

Cover and page design: orbitgraphic.co.uk

Printed and bound in Great Britain by Antony Rowe Limited in Chippenham, Wiltshire.

Contents

Marion

(1934-2002)

Publisher's Acknowledgements

Owing to the untimely death of the author shortly after the first draft of the book had been completed, had it not been for the for the work and dedication of a number of people, his text might never have seen the light of day. At the top of that list must be Alf Morris, The Rt Hon the Lord Morris of Manchester. His close attention to the array of factual details, in particular those relating to the process of enacting the Chronically Sick and Disabled Bill, which he drafted and piloted through Parliament, ensured the accuracy of this important book. Sir Richard Body, the former MP, not only played an important part in the success of that landmark Bill but also exerted his influence to ensure that the book was published. Next we must thank Dr Ian McKinlay OBE whose work with disabled people and more especially children with disabilities, made it highly appropriate for him to check the medical accuracy of the book. The author's son Simon Breed has also been very helpful and encouraging. Helen Carroll, our editor and proof- reader, and our typesetter, Lloyd Allen, put in an effort far beyond the demands of their jobs.

In a different category are the organisations which ensured the publication of the book. Neil Cawthorne of Temple Head introduced the book to the delegates at their conference and agreed to order a sufficient number of copies for publication to go ahead. Ken Carter of Defax contributed most of the illustrations and George Wilson used his influence very effectively. Joe Mann of the National League of the Blind and Disabled was also very encouraging and provided the photograph of their meeting with the Prime Minister in Trafalgar Square.

It is our intention after publication of the book to produce a booklet as a guide to the whole range of disability organisations to accompany the book, and all those wishing to be included are invited to send in brief details of their areas of work and how to contact them.

Alf Morris

Foreword

by The Rt Hon Lord Morris of Manchester AO QSO

Books are written for reasons innumerable and diverse. Some to fulfil an ambition or evict a bee from the author's bonnet to name but two. This book, from a highly readable author, is rooted in deep concern to make life better for disabled people.

Bryan Breed not only wrote about their problems and their needs: he had a long and enviable record of practical help in working to reduce the handicapping effects of their disabilities. For him precept and practice were as one. I speak in the past tense because, sadly and unexpectedly, Bryan died soon after his manuscript went to the publisher. Naturally his family and friends wanted publication to go ahead and we have here a book of considerable worth.

The history of disability is one of struggle against social exclusion and humiliation at their most cruel; but contrary to what many people think, it was not a process of gradual but inexorable social improvement across the centuries. For me the extreme example of where social exclusion can lead became startlingly clear when, not long after the Second World War, I stood among thousands upon thousands of rusting and rotting prostheses and wheelchairs, piled high in the dark fields of Auschwitz. They were the only remaining physical legacy of countless disabled people exterminated there as 'human refuse unworthy of life'. Bryan devoted a whole chapter to the hideous crimes against them. It demonstrates most graphically the depths to which inhumanity then sank.

In large parts of the world there was marked progress, over the last three decades of the twentieth century, in improving both the well-being and status of people with disabilities and social attitudes towards them. Yet even in the most advanced countries there remains a long unfinished agenda of unmet need, while in the world's poorest countries the lot of disabled people shames us all. The reason is starkly put in UNICEF'S report on '*The State of the World's Children*':

"When so much could be done for so many and at so little cost, then one central, shaming fact becomes unavoidable: these problems still exist not because the task is too large or too difficult or too expensive. It is because those most severely affected are almost exclusively the poorest and least politically influential people on earth."

Take the incidence of preventable blindness which has been falling in the developed world as dramatically as its incidence in most of the poorest countries has increased.

My involvement in disability began at birth, but became more purposeful when I entered the House of Commons in 1964, more especially when five years on I had the good fortune to win first place in the annual ballot for Private Members' Bills, and the right to propose a law of my own. The dour and, at times, seemingly hopeless battle to get my Chronically Sick and Disabled Persons Bill into law, against opposition from both sides of Parliament and extreme pressures of parliamentary time, is told in this book. The Bill's enactment in 1970 was described by a distinguished French disabled person as *un moment critique* for people with disabilities worldwide; and many of its provisions, notably those on access for disabled people to the built environment, were soon to be enacted by other Parliaments across the world.

That I would chose to legislate on disability was never in doubt. My father was severely disabled in the First World War and my earliest memories are of seeing him struggle even to breathe. He died – among the poorest of Manchester's poor in Ancoats – at the age of 44 in 1935 when I was seven years old.

The poverty and humiliation wrought by disability did not cease with his death. 'To help his family' the hospital where he died wanted to give him a pauper's burial directly from the mortuary. This deeply offended my mother and did not happen. But within two weeks she was told in what would now be called a word processed letter that, although my father had been a war pensioner, she had no entitlement to a war widow's pension because, said the War Office, he had died of 'heart failure' and not the war injuries for which his pension had been awarded.

This left me deeply aware of the unmerited and preventable suffering to which disabled people and their families were exposed and that addressing their problems and needs was the 'a' in etcetera of political priorities. By this I mean that whole parliaments came and went without any specific reference to the claims of disabled people. And at one General Election after another there was no mention whatever of disabled people in the manifesto of any political party. Nor was this true only of Britain. Nowhere in the world had disability ever figured prominently on any political agenda.

My awareness of the realities of life for people with disabilities was shared by the fellowship of parliamentarians who worked with me to enact the Chronically Sick and Disabled Persons Bill in 1970 as a first step on the legislative road to full citizenship for disabled people. Bryan Breed has analysed with immense care and insight the historical context in which this happened. Most of all he makes it plain that there is very much more to do to end preventable suffering among disabled people, even in the world's richest countries, and his book can help to quicken the pace of progress more widely.

I believe it will stand the test of time as a work of lasting value.

Disability

incapacity; inability; incapability; inherent lack; unfitness; impotence; helplessness; powerlessness; weakness; ineptitude; incompetence; disqualification; disablement; defect; afflictions; infirmity; handicap; impuissance; inanition; descrepitude; senility; superannuation; coduicity; paralysis; collapse; exhaustion.

Disable

indispose; incapacitate; cripple; lame; prostrate; mutilate; mangle; impair; mar; spoil; make harmless

Longmans Synonym Dictionary

Introduction

As can be seen from the Longman's synonyms even the language makes villains of disabled people, turning human beings into caricatures, people of courage and strength into weaklings and models of impotence and helplessness. Language mirrors life, and it is obvious that social attitudes, especially bias, are encapsulated within it. There is little there which goes beyond the unimportant outward trappings of disability to recognise the abilities of the human being within.

If this book does have abiding meaning, it must be about such social attitudes. It cannot be a mere collection of historical details. It must trace the path by which disabled people have come from being objects of derision and fear through to the beginnings of activism and empowerment. It is not meant to be a comprehensive history: it would have been impossible to go down every fascinating pathway which presented itself, or to trace the story of every type of disability and every organisation involved. In advance, apologies are made to those organisations which have made a contribution to the advancement of disabled people but about which no mention is made here. It would have been impossible to mention them all.

This book deals with the lives of disabled people and, most importantly, public attitudes towards them, through the centuries until that day in Britain in 1970 when, in a race against time with only two days of a Parliament remaining, the Chronically Sick and Disabled Persons Bill became law. It started a remarkable process of change and improvement, first in Britain and then across the world.

This book reflects those changes, and tells of the progress made towards pinpointing the causes and prevention of some disabilities. Importantly, it recounts how the improvements have not only enabled disabled people to lead fuller lives but to become activists themselves with a good, strong voice which augurs well for gaining all that still needs to be achieved. The exciting additional story – told in chapter 15 – is of how the impetus created in 1970 by the UK's new and landmark legislation for disabled people became the model for world improvement.

However, those who have seen those improvements in the lot of disabled people, here and in other richly endowed countries, should not get carried away. There are still huge areas of the world where the winds of change have not even rustled the leaves on the trees, where people suffer disability because simple methods of prevention costing very little cannot be afforded by their communities, and where disability, once it is in place, is seldom alleviated because that would be beyond the means of the community in which they live.

Some Important Dates

The Rig-Veda, a collection of sacred Indian poems, contains the first written record of a prosthesis. Written in Sanskrit between **3500** and **1800 BC** it records the story of a warrior Queen Vishpla who lost her leg in battle and was fitted with an iron prosthesis, and returned to battle.

355 BC Aristotle wrote 'those born deaf become speechless and incapable of reason'.

218 BC Marcus Segius, Roman general who led his legion against Carthage in 2nd Punic War, sustained 23 injuries and had a right arm amputated. An iron hand was made to hold his shield, and he was able to return to battle. He was afterwards denied the opportunity to be a priest because he had to be whole with two normal hands.

590 AD Romans made the first recorded provision to care for 'cripples'. Pope Gregory included them in his classification of infirm and destitute to be supported by public funds.

15th century humanistic scholar Roelof Huysman (1444-1485) wrote *De Formando Studio* which contains a description of a person deaf from birth who acquired the ability to read and write, a refutation of conventional dogma that nothing could be done to alleviate the condition.

16th century Girolamo Gardano (1501-1576) was the first physician to recognise the ability of deaf people to reason, and, citing Roelof Huysman's account (above), proposed the revolutionary view that deaf persons were educable.

1508 Gotz von Berlichingen, German Knight, lost his arm at the Battle of Laudsshut in 1508. He had two mechanical iron hands made. Each joint could be moved and relaxed by setting a release spring. The hand could pronate and supinate and was suspended with leather straps.

1543 Publication of '*De humani corporis fabrica*', the first real anatomical atlas, by Andreas Vesalius

1578 French physician Laurent Joubert published '*Erreurs Populaires*' exposing popular fallacies about the causes of illness and disability.

1600 The first microscope constructed by three Dutch spectacle makers, Hans Hanssen, his son Zacharias, and Hans Lipperskey.

Blind poet John Milton (1608-74) created the awareness that blind people can be creative.

1616 G.Bonifacio published a treatise discussing sign language. '*Of the Art of Signs*'

1628 Publication of '*De Motu Cordis*', which demonstrated the circulation of the blood, by William Harvey.

1696 Pieter Andriannszoon Verduyn, Dutch surgeon, introduced first history of disability .

Renaissance book – '*De re Medicina*.'

18th century saw the beginnings of a revival of Hippocrates' enlightened attitude to mental disorders. The belief in witches and diabolic possession was decreasing: it was no longer automatically assumed that lunatics were possessed by the devil or by the moon, but in the absence of any satisfactory explanation for their actions they were cruelly treated.

18th century saw the coming together of a number of 'blind emancipators' in England who were influential in establishing the nation's first schools for blind pupils.

French oculist Jacques Daviel (1696-1762) found a method of removing cataracts.

1754 First trials to overcome scurvy were started.

1755 First deaf school established in Germany by Samuel Heinicke. Charles Michel Abbe del Epee in Paris established the first free school for deaf children in the world.

1760 Thomas Braidwood opened first school for deaf pupils in England. Italy had its first such school in Rome.

1774 Madhouse Act in England set up rudimentary licensing and certification of asylums with magistrates empowered to carry out writs.

Previously, the 18th century madhouse had been a secret place, hidden away from public scrutiny. Reforms proposed in England met opposition from vested medical interests who feared profitability of private asylums would be threatened.

1790 The Frenchman Philippe Pinel unshackled people suffering from mental illness at the Bicetre Asylum in Paris.

1796 Edward Jenner undertook first vaccination against smallpox using cowpox.

In England patient numbers in asylums rose from a few thousands in 1800 to some 100,000 in 1900. By the last third of the 19th century statistics had demonstrated the expectation that asylums would prove effective as a 'cure' were unfounded. Sterilisation of those with physical and mental disabilities and problems continued to be a widespread practice well into the 1970s.

1801 Pinel published his Medico-philosophical Treatment on Mental Alienation.

1805 Rush's *Medical Inquiries and Observations* was the first modern attempt to explain mental disorders.

1809 Louis Braille born.

1829 Braille invented raised print alphabet.

1851 Census counted 409,207 cases of deformity in Britain

1851 First 'modern' artificial limbs displayed at the Crystal Palace Exhibition.

1860 Pasteur demonstrated that micro-organisms were a reality.

1867 Joseph Lister published the results of research which showed that carbolic acid killed infections.

1872 Alexander Graham Bell opened a speech school for teachers of the deaf.

1882 Robert Koch isolated the micro-organism responsible for tuberculosis.

1883 Koch isolated cholera micro-organism.

1890 Karl Fraenkel developed vaccine against diphtheria.

1895 Joseph Lister introduced diphtheria vaccine into Britain.

1907 Paul Ehrlich developed the first effective treatment for syphilis, Salvarsan.

1921 Fred Banting and Charles Best produced the first insulin which could be used to treat diabetes.

1921 Alexander Fleming discovered penicillin, the first antibiotic.

1932 Gerhard Domagk created the first effective treatment against streptococci caused diseases, Prontosil. It overcame gonorrhoea, meningitis, urinary tract infection, and mastoiditis.

1933 A.J. Ewins developed Sulfadiazine which could kill pneumococcal infections and thus proved effective against pneumonia.

1939 The Aktion T-4 Programme began in Germany, which killed over 70,000 disabled children and adults in hospitals and institutions.

1941 Norman Heatley and Andrew Myser developed a method of producing penicillin in quantity.

1943 Penicillin at last began to be produced in quantity by drug companies and became available as the first effective antibiotic.

1955 Jonas Salk developed the first successful polio vaccine.

1970 Chronically Sick and Disabled Persons Act became law in Britain after Alf Morris MP had introduced the legislation in a Private Member's Bill.

1970 John Charnley performed the first successful hip replacement at Manchester Royal Infirmary.

1970 Barbara Ansell developed the first effective method of managing children with Juvenile Chronic Arthritis, or Stills Disease, to help them overcome the disease with little or no residual damage to their growth and limbs.

1974 Britain appointed the world's first Government Minister for Disabled People.

1974–79 The introduction of wide-ranging financial help for disabled people in Britain by statutory right.

1980 Rehabilitation International's *Charter of the 1980s*

1994 Professor Tiny Maini's research leads to first anti-TNF (tumour necrosis factor) drug effectively to combat rheumatoid arthritis.

1995 Disability Discrimination Act passed

2000 Rehabilitation International's *Charter for the New Millennium*

2007 United Nations convention on the rights of Disabled People, envisaged by the Charter, approved by the U.N. General Assembly.

Chapter One

The Middle Ages and Onwards

From the sixteenth Century in Western society a growing knowledge of the body and the science of medicine saw the blossoming of a new 'scientific age', but this still went hand in hand with the belief that supernatural forces may also be involved in causing sickness and disability. There was still much ignorance; French physician Laurent Joubert (1529-83) denounced the beliefs held by many medical men about pregnancy and childbirth. One of the most widely held was that when babies were born with birthmarks it was because they had been conceived at the time of menstruation. Joubert said, on the contrary, that he believed it was impossible that a woman should conceive during her menstrual flow. Another superstition was that whatever the mother was imagining at the time of conception would shape the birthmark.

Disabled people were still feared. It was fundamental to how they were perceived and treated in the middle-ages and the Renaissance, and it resulted in their being isolated in the alms houses, where most of them were also put to work. They were not perceived as a group distinct from the poor.

Paracelsus, the name adopted by the Swiss Philippus Aureolus Bombastus von Hohenheim who lived from 1493 to 1542, is often credited with being the father of a new scientific approach to disabilities, but even he associated disease with nymphs, gnomes and

'germs' falling from the heavens. However, one of his major contributions came from his interest in the health problems of mine
workers which led to his investigating the role of chemical agents.
This, in turn, caused him to investigate cretinism, prevalent in
the valleys of Switzerland, and he was the first to associate the
condition with retardation. He also was the first to recognise the
variable nature of retardation. Another who helped shift opinion
was Ambroise Parc (1517-90) who introduced the concept of
hereditary disability to offer arguments against disabilities being
caused by demonology.

A doctor who was also a clergyman, Richard Napier, a
graduate of Oxford University who died in 1634, treated sick and
disabled people with the medicines then available but would still
pray that they be protected from evil spirits, fairies and witches.
Indeed, the Church never discouraged the belief of many of its
parishioners that rituals, particularly the Holy Communion, had
healing and protective qualities. It was also widely believed that
disability and illness could be transferred. This could be to the
dead, by touching a dead person, or to an object. In the latter case
the object, be it a stone, a cloth, or even another animal, which
came into contact with the disability would be buried.

In England at the time of the Civil War, Nicholas Culpeper, a
former apprentice to an apothecary, went on to set himself up as
a doctor to the London poor. He not only translated the College
of Physicians' Latin *Pharmacopoeia*, but produced his own
version of cheap herbal remedies which later became known as
Culpeper's Herbal. This contained five hundred plant remedies to
deal with all human sicknesses and disabilities. The College was
not amused, but Culpeper maintained that the poor were entitled
to treatment, particularly because its cost was being driven up by
physicians through the mystique they maintained by continuing
to use Latin.

The sixteenth and seventeenth centuries saw no great improvement in the treatment of disabilities, but there was certainly
no reduction in the number of different people available to help
overcome them: physicians, herbalists, wise women, astrologers,

apothecaries, and barber-surgeons. Some very strange 'medicines' continued to be used: frog spawn, senna powder, cinnamon, nutmeg, and blood transfusions from dogs and sheep. Medical investigation and progress began to improve a little with the beginning of the Age of Enlightenment from the 1700s onwards and with it the insistence on a more scientific approach, but with little agreement about what precise form this should take. Moreover, it was difficult to find evidence that this approach resulted in better clinical practice. In the mid- eighteenth century an Englishman lived on average thirty-six years, whilst in France the figure was only twenty-seven years. The best doctors were now making a great deal of money in London treating the rich and the famous. Only a few, among them John Coakley Lettsom (1744-1815) who earned around £12,000 a year, strayed from their lucrative practices to help the poor. Lettsom wrote papers advocating lying-in, helping the deaf and dumb, dispensaries, and even cheap porridge for the poor. On the whole a bedside manner continued to be more valued by the well-to-do patients than actual clinical skills. The lower classes dealt with sickness and disability themselves, for this was all they could afford. To help them a 'poor man's' literature of cheap and easy remedies sprung up. Preacher and founder of Methodism John Wesley wrote his *Primitive Physick* in 1747 which was immensely popular. In it he advocated using ingredients available to ordinary people: onions, honey, liquorice, and even goose droppings for baldness.

This treatise was followed by William Buchan's *Domestic Medicine* (1769) and the *Poor Man's Medicine Chest*, author unrecorded, in 1791. Alongside this treat-yourself-because-nobody-else-will approach developed a whole world of quackery, with cheap potions being offered to overcome everything from rheumatic problems and loss of potency, to venereal disease and cancer.

However, medical discoveries were in truth leading to a better understanding of some conditions and disabilities, and this led to a better attitude towards those afflicted by them. Battista Morgagni, professor of anatomy at Padua, whose work reporting how disease left tell-tale marks on the internal body was translated into English in 1769, showed that apoplexy or stroke was not the result of a lesion in the brain but alteration in the brain's blood vessels. In other words, many types of disability and illness could now be explained through changes found in the internal organs of the body, and not by strange or supernatural intervention. Although there was now a greater understanding of disease and resulting disability, there were not as yet ways of treating much of it.

Blood-letting and purging were still common practice when there was little else that could be done. Taking the waters at spas like Bath, Buxton, Cheltenham to name but a few, became fashionable to ease or overcome severe disabilities which it was obvious would require more than water to relieve. At Bath there is archeological evidence that people living around the hot water spring were throwing offerings into the water 8000 years B C. In AD 43 the Romans started to develop Aquas Sulis as a healing sanctuary and a place of relaxation. After the Romans left, the baths and the accompanying temple became ruins, but in the 11th century, the King's Bath was built over the spring as part of an infirmary. In the 12th century the St.John's Hospital was built on the site using the baths to treat disability. Years later Queen Anne started a craze when she visited and took to the waters in 1692, 1702 and 1703, and over two hundred spas sprung up which continued to prosper as centres of treatment and rehabilitation for disabled people for over two centuries.

It was logical that extolling the virtues of sea water would follow from the success of the spas in the 17th and 18th centuries. Dr. Richard Russell (1687-1759) made Brighton famous by insisting not only that people would benefit from bathing in the sea but also by drinking from it.

In the 1920s many war wounded were rehabilitated in Bath and in spas throughout the country. In 1948 the last ten spas came under the control of the NHS, and taking the waters became part of the treatment for the relief of a whole range of ailments, but particularly arthritis and rheumatism. After a girl died in 1978, her death thought to be caused by amoeba contaminating the Bath spring, the natural baths became a museum, never used for treatments. In 2003, however, a new bore hole was sunk about a hundred yards from the source, and a fresh new spa opened. It seems that our ancestors knew something by instinct which we are only beginning to prove through science. Studies have shown that baths containing radon gas can relieve the symptoms and disabilities caused by rheumatoid arthritis and ankylosing spondylitis, according to a Dutch trial reported in the journal *Arthritis and Rheumatism*. Another trial published in the *New England Journal of Medicine* indicates that soaking in a spa for thirty minutes a day can reduce blood glucose levels.

In 18th and 19th centuries, there was a growing trend towards stuffing patients full of pills and potions, mainly to convince them that something was being offered for their pain and problems. The result was a growth in drug-making companies to meet the demand, with herbs forming the main basis of most of what they produced. Whatever they were, their effects were largely emetic or laxative. There were exceptions. One Edmund Stone, who died in 1768, observed that willow bark reduced the symptoms of ague or fever, even in those with rheumatic fever. Of course, willow bark is a source of aspirin, a fact long known by, for instance, native American Indians.

In 1785 William Withering published an account of his use of foxglove, or digitalis, and its use in treating dropsy and heart disease. When it appeared eight years later in the *Pharmacopoeia Edinburgensis* and then twenty-six years later in the *London Pharmacopoeia* it became widely used and relieved and prevented much disability.

There was one area of disease and disability against which definite progress was made: the great killer and disfigurer, smallpox, responsible at one time for about a tenth of all deaths in Europe. The first human inoculation of variolous material, or variolation, goes back to very ancient times, and most oriental people knew about its potentials. The first hints in the Western world that it was possible to immunise against disease came from a strange source: Lady Mary Wortley Montagu, wife of the British Consul in Constantinople. In 1717 she wrote to a friend in England reporting that Turkish peasant women regularly organised smallpox parties at which they performed what could only be described as inoculations. At these, veins were opened and a small amount of smallpox pus was introduced on the head of a needle, thus promoting a mild dose of the disease from which the one inoculated easily recovered but which then appeared to give lifelong protection. In England Sir Hans Sloane became a pioneer inoculator. When Lady Mary Wortley Montagu returned she went to the surgeon Charles Maitland to have her five-year-old daughter inoculated. Experiments were then undertaken on condemned prisoners. Other trial inoculations followed in the community. Surgeons Robert Sutton and his sons devised an easy and safe method of administering inoculations, and over a thirty year period they gave this preventive treatment to 400,000 people. There was some risk and a small number of deaths, because, after all, the smallpox itself was being used as the inoculatory agent. Because of the risk and because it was considered unnatural by many, smallpox still killed a thirteenth of each generation.

It was a country doctor called Edward Jenner who removed both the risk and the distrust by discovering a safer form of the vaccination. He noticed that a disease of cattle, called cowpox was occasionally caught by humans but, benignly, appeared to give the sufferers immunity against smallpox. In 1796 he was ready to begin vaccinating humans. An eight-year-old boy named James Phipps was given cowpox pus taken from the hand of Sarah Nelmes, a dairy maid. The lad suffered a little fever, but soon got over that. A few weeks later Jenner inoculated the boy with smallpox, which did not develop, proving that cowpox could be used as a safer way of immunising against the deadly disease. By 1798 he had 23 recorded cases, and he published his findings in a paper named *An Inquiry into the Causes and Effects of Variola Vaccina*. His method became widely used throughout Europe and America. In Holland and Prussia vaccination was made compulsory and in those countries smallpox was eradicated. Sadly, such is world poverty that it was only in 1997, through the efforts of the World Health Organisation, that the disease was eradicated on a global scale. Perhaps more importantly, it led to a curiosity about which other diseases could be overcome by immunisation. In 1803 the Royal Jennerian Society was set up to promote vaccination, indicating that at last prevention was being recognised as better than cure.

At about the same time as Jenner was making his observations on smallpox, a young obstetrician named Alexander Gordon working in Aberdeen was researching Puerperal Fever, a type of blood poisoning which killed mothers following childbirth. He came to two conclusions: one that it was related to erysipelas, also known as St.Anthony's fire, and secondly, that it was being transmitted to women during childbirth by the doctors and midwives assisting them. During his published descriptions of twenty-eight cases he studied, he confessed that he himself had been responsible for unwittingly transmitting the infection and also named several midwives. His frankness led to great unpopularity among his medical colleagues and he had to leave and join the navy, where he died of tuberculosis at the age of 48. Fortunately, his earlier investigations led to Oliver Wendell Holmes undertaking research into the same disease and to a published paper in 1843. This showed that cleanliness could help prevent transmission, but the main progress in eradicating Puerperal Fever did not come until 1935 when Leonard Colebrook showed that using sulphanilanide reduced mortality to almost nil.

There was also some progress made against blindness. As always, cataracts were a major cause of disability. It became known that this condition was caused by the hardening of the lens of the eye. The French oculist Jacques Daviel (1696-1762) discovered that he could successfully remove the damaged lens to reprieve the sufferer's sight, and the technique spread rapidly.

Perhaps the most hopeful trend came from the growing realisation that disease could be attacked long before a dramatic cure was identified. The first controlled trials aimed at overcoming scurvy took place on HMS Salisbury in 1754. Previously, scurvy, together with dysentery, were the major causes of death in the British navy. Scurvy was investigated by a Scottish naval surgeon called James Lind. Although Lind saw orange and lemon juice as a source of treatment for the disease, it later became apparent that people eating these, and other fresh fruit and vegetables, did not get the disease in the first place. After the general issue of lemon juice to sailors in 1795, scurvy to all intent and purposes disappeared from the British navy. Grog became a cold toddy of rum, water and citrus juice from 1795 on.

Another Scotsman named John Pringle pursued research which drew attention to the role of 'contagion' in diseases like 'gaol fever' – typhus. He attacked insanitary conditions in the army and in prisons. He was Physician General to the army from 1742 until 1758 and then went on to investigate conditions in prisons. Pringle advocated that the best way of preventing gaol fever was to burn prisoners' old clothes on their arrival, that new clothes be supplied and the bodies they adorned should be washed from 'time to time'. He pinpointed the need for hygiene and good public health measures. John Howard (1749-1834) took up the baton to call for hygienic reform in hospitals. After visits to such establishments in Britain and on the continent he concluded that dirt and unventilated atmospheres were responsible for many fevers, including typhus.

Although it may seem obvious to us now from these accounts that infection was a major source of disease and disability in society, it appeared to take an extraordinarily long time for the penny to drop in places where it mattered above all others: the operating theatre and the hospital ward. Long before, the unfortunate Alexander Gordon had been the first to make a link between Puerperal Fever, which killed many mothers after childbirth, and infection by suggesting that putrid matter from the midwife or doctor was responsible. He recommended thorough washing by those attending births, but was drummed out of the medical profession for his trouble.

Because of a failure to overcome infection, mainly because there was no real understanding about what caused it, sepsis was so widespread in hospitals that gangrene was almost routine after, operations, leading to disability and all too frequently subsequent death. Those who survived usually only did so without the use of at least one limb. It was the pursuit of Alexander Gordon's early observations about the source of Puerperal Fever, or childbed fever, that provided most clues. In America Oliver Wendell Holmes(1809-94) similarly believed that it was caused by an infection, transmitted by those attending the birth, but was rebutted by other medical men thought to be more experienced. In the 1840s in Vienna, Ignaz Semmelweis observed that childbed fever raged in one ward in which birth was assisted by medical students, but was practically non-existent in another maternity ward served by midwifery pupils. The only reason he could think of was that the medical students were more in touch with infection. His point was proved when a colleague, Jacob Kolletschka, died after cutting his finger during an autopsy. Semmelweis found changes in his body identical to those found in the bodies of the women who died of childbed fever. He concluded that medical students often came directly from autopsies and were carrying the cause of the infection with them. In 1847 Semmelweis made washing the hands with chlorinated water compulsory before assisting with deliveries, and cases of childbed fever decreased considerably. He still met resistance from colleagues who resented his suppositions.

This is surprising because even the Greeks had used wine and vinegar to safeguard wounds, and later alcohol and iodine came into use as early antiseptics.

Despite these findings, there was still a reluctance to take infection seriously. It was Joseph Lister (1827-1912), a Yorkshire surgeon working in Edinburgh, who came up with a solution. During his research, Lister found that Louis Pasteur had suggested that micro-organisms were responsible for infection. He next noted that carbolic acid reduced infection in cattle, and that it was extensively used to treat sewage. He first tried it in August 1865 when he dressed with lint soaked in carbolic acid and linseed oil the wound of a boy who had been run over by a cart. The wound stayed infection free. Lister continued to use and develop the technique. He then extended the principle into the operating theatre, spraying the atmosphere with carbolic before and during the operation. Lister published his results in a medical journal in March 1867, but suffered a sceptical response from those who still denied the existence of bacteria. Nevertheless, his method was taken up by others in Europe to great effect. It was not, however, until Robert Koch's (1843-1910) researches showed not only the existence but the specific role of micro-organisms that 'Listerism', as it was named, really triumphed. There was still a long way to go: even Lister operated in his street clothes, and nobody thought of wearing sanitised operating gowns and rubber gloves until much later. Despite the fact that carbolic acid was abandoned, even by Lister himself, the principle that sterilisation was essential had been established, and much death and disability avoided.

Aside from medical advances, there was little change in attitudes towards disabled people until the First World War. A new way, both cultural and social, of addressing disability appears to have had its seeds in those left disabled by the conflict. It was principally the idea of rehabilitation and reintegration, and this resulted in the first combined actions of a medical, therapeutic, and social nature directed at disabled people. The real development of the prosthesis dates from the war: before that only the crutch and wooden leg were available.

Chapter Two

The Battle Against the Causes of Disability

If the 18th century was the age of do-it-yourself treatment with herbal remedies, with the poor and disabled people unable to afford to consult a physician, the first half of the 19th century saw the growth of primary care. Physicians had been available to the well-to-do for some time, but gradually they began to see that they had a duty also to treat those who were poorer. Charities and friendly societies, by providing some of the finance needed, together with the development of charitable hospitals, helped the growing trend. Although doctors became available they had very little in their medical armoury with which to treat disease or prevent avoidable disability. Infection was widespread, with diseases like chickenpox, measles, diphtheria, scarlet fever, gastro-intestinal illnesses, dysentery, tuberculosis, syphilis, meningitis and sepsis, causing early deaths to millions of children and adults, and life-long disability to many who survived. Doctors could only reassure and prescribe bed rest, tonics, purging with laxatives, and blood letting. There were just a few ailments against which more effective methods were available: mercury for ring worm and syphilis, digitalis for the weak heart, amylnitrate for angina, quinine for malaria and colchicene for gout. In terms of chronic conditions, nothing was available to combat diabetes, arthritis, asthma or heart disease. Soothing the patient became the order of the day. Fortunately the growing chemical industry was happy to oblige and produced strong sedatives, pain killers and narcotic drugs. Many had an alcoholic base, and opium was also freely available. Thankfully, the horizons of primary care were about to be expanded through new curiosity about micro-organisms. The theory that disease was passed from one person to another by tiny, invasive organisms was far from new. Girolamo Frascastoro had written in 1546 of 'seminaria contagiosa', or disease seeds. Others had investigated what caused decay in food and bodies. Theories that invasive organisms caused specific diseases gained strength in the nineteenth century, but there was still a great deal of scepticism and controversy.

It was Louis Pasteur, a chemist who became interested in biology, who produced the first evidence. In 1854 he was appointed to a Chair in the University at Lille and began to research fermentation. It was his belief that fermentation was the result of particular living micro-organisms. His investigations continued when he took up a Chair in Paris, and by 1860 he had established that fermentation needed micro-organisms which were not dependent on oxygen. He then developed ingenious experimental methods to demonstrate that these same micro-organisms were in the air. Next he showed that heat would kill them. Pasteur, inevitably, turned his attention to the relationship between micro-organisms and disease and rotting. He also demonstrated that killing micro-organisms, by heating, in wine, beer and milk, purified them. Hence pasteurization was born. In 1878 Pasteur argued the case for infection through micro-organisms in front of the French Academy of Medicine. Later that year, together with Jules Joubert and Charles Chamberland, he published a paper which made the case that only particular organisms could make specific diseases. It indicated that once these organisms had been isolated and made known, prevention was a distinct possibility, perhaps by developing vaccines. Through a striking series of scientific demonstrations he showed that he could successfully vaccinate chickens against a disease called chicken cholera and cattle against anthrax. Helped again by

Chamberland and a scientist called Pierre Emile Roux, Pasteur transferred his attention to rabies. He was unable to find the microbe which caused it, but nevertheless continued his quest to find a vaccine for this too. In 1884 he made a series of experiments which indicated that his vaccine saved animals from rabies. His opportunity to demonstrate that it would also save humans came dramatically in July 1885 when a nine-year-old boy, Joseph Meister, was brought to him. The unfortunate child had been bitten fifteen times by a rabid dog. Reacting to a plea from the boy's mother, Pasteur gave him a series of increasingly strong injections over fourteen days: the boy did not get rabies. Three months later a fourteen-year-old shepherd, Jean-Baptiste Jupille, who had been attacked by a rabid dog, was vaccinated with the same positive outcome. The procedure was quickly taken up, with some 20,000 at risk people being vaccinated over the next ten years.

Building on Pasteur's work, Robert Koch (1843-1910), who had already begun investigations into micro-organisms involved in anthrax at about the same time as the French scientist, turned bacteriology into a discipline. It was he who established the germ concept of disease. In March 1882 Koch was able to reveal his mycobacterium tuberculosis, the organism causing tuberculosis. A year later he isolated vibrio cholerae during field research in Egypt. He journeyed on to India to demonstrate the following year that this cholera-causing agent lived in the human intestine and was passed on to other humans through polluted water. Pupils of Koch went on to pinpoint the micro-organisms causing the streptococcal and staphylococcal infections tetanus, syphilis, gonorrhoea, meningitis, pneumonia, diphtheria, typhoid, leprosy, and whooping cough.

Unfortunately, having identified the micro-organisms involved, success in developing vaccines in some diseases proved elusive. It was not until 1890 that a German, Karl Fraenkel, showed that the weakened cultures of diphtheria bacilli brought immunity from the disease.

Emil Behring and Shibasaburo Kitasato demonstrated that

the blood of such an immune animal could be used to treat a second animal who had been exposed to this deadly disease. The first child with diphtheria received this serum on Christmas Day 1891 in Berlin. It was then widely used in Germany with success. Joseph Lister brought the diphtheria serum into use in England in 1895, and the mortality rate dropped. Immunisation was now possible on a huge scale through animal serum.

However, other bacterially induced diseases proved difficult to inoculate against. This set off the search in the field of chemotherapy to find a drug that would overcome micro-organisms. Paul Ehrlich (1854-1915) of Frankfurt-am-Main began investigating antibodies – the proteins produced by the body's own defence system to fight disease – with the idea of producing these artificially in the laboratory to combat specific diseases. He set out to develop chemical, tailor-made antibodies, and first turned his attention to dyes. Ehrlich tried an aniline dye, methylene blue, on malaria, with promising results. He tried another drug, atoxyl, an arsenical compound, on sleeping sickness, but the side effects were far from beneficial.

His next target was syphilis. By 1907 he had tested over six hundred arsenical compounds, and number 606 looked promising. Two years later, working with a Japanese bacteriologist, Shachiro Hata, Ehrlich retested 606 and found it to be effective. After two doctors had themselves acted as guinea pigs, they gave 606 to some of their patients and these showed great improvements. 606 was developed by a drug company as Salvarsan, and transformed treatment for this stubborn disease.

Sadly researchers had no such luck when seeking chemotherapeutic answers to many other bacterial diseases, and it was not until 1935 that a further breakthrough was made. Gerhard Domagk (1895-1964) set out to test the effectiveness of metal-based compounds against micro-organisms. He found none that was satisfactory. When he became research director to a chemical company whose main products were dyes he turned his focus to researching whether these had any effect on streptococci. In 1932 he discovered that one red dye, an azo-compound called

Prontosil, overcame streptococci in mice. His faith in Prontosil became so strong that he used it to treat his own daughter for an infection. The Pasteur Institute in France verified Domagk's work, and discovered more about Prontosil's mode of action. They showed that the compound divided into two parts in the body and that one of the parts, subsequently named sulphanilamide, was responsible for its success in combating streptococci. It did not actually kill bacteria, rather it stopped them from multiplying within the body, and this allowed the body's own defence system to recover and overcome them. Prontosil quickly became widely available. It was particularly effective against Puerperal Fever: when used at a maternity hospital in London it brought mortality rates down from 20 to 4.7 per cent. It could overcome gonorrhoea in five days, and was effective against mastoiditis, meningitis, and many urinary tract infections. Domagk received the Nobel Prize for his research.

Pneumococcal infections resisted Prontosil stubbornly, and so others turned their attention to finding similar compounds which might treat them. A.J.Ewins, working for May and Baker, came up with sulfadiazine 693 which was proved to work against pneumococci, and was even more effective than Prontosil against streptococci.

Sulfadiazine and Prontosil became the magic bullets of the doctor's black bag, but they became over-prescribed. Strains of streptococci resistant to the new sulpha drugs appeared. Despite this they not only remained a very helpful weapon against bacterial diseases, but also encouraged more research to find other anti-bacterial agents which could be used.

This is where the legendary Alexander Fleming came in. Pasteur's earlier research had shown that biological agents could destroy micro-organisms. Paul Vuillemin (1861-1932) had described the way in which one creature destroys the life of another to preserve its own, as antibiosis. Fleming, building on earlier work in this area of investigation, in 1921 identified an enzyme called lysozyme, which came from tears and mucous fluids, as part of the body's own defence mechanism. An accidental contamination of a culture by nasal mucus showed that it had powers to destroy bacteria. A second accident led to the discovery of penicillin. Six years later he was researching staphylococci, which cause carbuncles, boils, pneumonia and septicaemia, when he went on holiday. On his return he found that a mould which had formed on a staphylococcus culture left in a dish in his Paddington, London, laboratory appeared to have killed off the staphylococcus colonites it had contained. He identified the mould as Penicillium Rubrum, although it was actually Penicillium Notatum. Importantly, he went on to show that it destroyed a whole range of the bacteria causing infections but appeared to have no side-effects. Unfortunately, Fleming found it difficult to produce the Penicillium, which meant that he could not develop a method of gathering it in the quantity that would make it useful clinically. Although Fleming published his findings, the scientific community paid little attention, and his work on Penicillium stopped there.

It was a full ten years later that scientists in Oxford, led by Howard Florey and helped considerably by biochemist Ernst Chain, began a research project on microbial antagonisms, and came across Fleming's paper. They attempted to grow Penicillium Notatum, but had the same trouble as Fleming. Fortunately, they persisted and another biochemist in the team, Norman Heatley, improved production techniques, though still finding it difficult to produce enough to be of any real use. They did get enough to show, in mice, experiments that penicillin was very effective against potentially fatal streptococcal infections. They next treated a patient near to death from staphylococcal septaemia. He was making a remarkable recovery until the fourth day when the supply of penicillin ran out and he died. It was at this point that Florey turned to the drug companies to ask for their help to produce penicillin in quantity. The British companies, at that time obsessed with keeping up with the demands for medicines created by the Second World War, were too busy to pay attention, so in July 1941 he turned to the United States. Heatley went over to work with Andrew Myer of the Northern Regional Research Laboratory in Illinois and together they raised the penicillin yield thirty-four-fold. American pharmaceutical companies were delighted to produce the new wonder drug, followed by British companies in 1943. Fleming, Florey and Chain received the 1945 Nobel prize for their work. Other antibiotics followed rapidly, particularly streptomycin, which proved effective against tuberculosis. Thus treatments were now available against bacteria, micro-organisms which had for centuries caused illness, disability and death.

Conditions caused by viruses have proved harder to tackle. Isolation and identification of viral agents began in the late nineteenth century when Chamberland developed a filter which separated bacteria from viruses. Viral diseases became identified successfully, and then the hunt was on for vaccines to combat them. A leading figure in the chase was the American John Enders, who managed to grow viruses in animal tissues. In March 1948 Enders produced mumps viruses in culture, and a year later polio virus on human tissue. Enders produced a measles vaccine, licensed in 1963.

It was Jonas Salk, following a polio epidemic responsible for 50,000 new cases a year in the United States, who developed the first effective vaccine against this killing and disabling viral agent. In 1935 a weak vaccine had been tested in 17,000 children in the United States but this not only proved ineffective but led to twelve of those injected directly developing polio. Salk chose a killed virus vaccine, and, after successful preliminary tests, used it in trials which involved two million children. In April 1955 the results showed that the Salk vaccine was safe.

Developing drugs, as distinct from vaccines, against viruses has proved difficult. It was well into the nineteen-seventies before drugs were developed to combat shingles and herpes. Interferon has proved to be an elusive agent, but it has been shown to be effective against multiple sclerosis. Attempts to find drugs to combat influenza have proved abortive, though vaccines are prepared each year.

The balance sheet of prevention of death and early treatment of disability has dramatically changed over the last hundred years.

Effective vaccines have been developed against many diseases. Drugs have been produced to arrest and relieve the symptoms of others. Among those in the latter category are most of the major chronic disabling diseases such as arthritis, diabetes, some heart conditions, kidney and liver diseases, and cancer. Although these continue to plague mankind some progress is being made against them.

The rheumatic diseases have always been a major cause of disability. They have been identified in the bones of the skeletons of the Nubian slaves who provided the labour for building the pyramids. They remain one of the world's leading causes of disability: when Amelia Harris completed the first ever survey of impairment in the UK in the seventies, the rheumatic diseases accounted for two-thirds of all disability.

In the case of rheumatoid arthritis, researchers at the Mayo Clinic in America thought they had found the answer in the 1930s when they investigated the use of cortisone, or steroids. These also proved highly effective against other inflammatory conditions. It was finally used to treat patients after the Second World War with quite spectacular success. Rheumatoid arthritis sufferers in the United States, literally, took up their beds and walked for the first time in years. Unfortunately, shortly after its first use the side effects became startlingly obvious. Doses given were too large and patients developed heart conditions, skin disorders, stomach bleeding and ulcers. Not surprisingly cortisone quickly went out of fashion until the fourth quarter of the twentieth century when physicians learnt to use it in smaller doses to achieve results over a longer period of time. It is now effectively used still in severe rheumatoid arthritis and in another rheumatic disease called polymyalgia rheumatica, which does not attack the actual joints but the soft tissues around them. However, the main progress in combating rheumatoid arthritis has been in better management of the disease using Non-Steroidal Anti-Inflammatory (NSAID) and other drugs to deal with the inflammation which damages and erodes the cartilage and bone in joints. Real progress has been made, much of it through research financed by the research charity formerly known as the Arthritis & Rheumatism Council and now called the Arthritis Research Campaign, which developed after the Second World War under the leadership of an imaginative lay General Secretary, Michael Andrews, CBE.

In recent years research has been helped by the discovery that rheumatoid arthritis is an auto-immune disease, one in which the body's defence mechanism attacks its own tissues in the joints. This has led to the discovery and use of a range of drugs which interferes with the mechanism of this attack. Most outstanding in this area has been the work of Professor Tiny Maini, of the Kennedy Institute of Rheumatology, London, who found ways of interfering with the auto-immune process by identifying a chemical messenger, TNF (tumour necrosis factor) which made it happen. He then went on to develop, with Professor Marc Feldman, anti-TNF drugs.

The same good management has helped children who had previously been crippled and their growth stunted by a childhood form of a similar rheumatic disease called Still's Disease, better known now as Juvenile Chronic Arthritis. One of the British pioneers was the physician Barbara Ansell, who died in 2001, and who treated children first at the Canadian Red Cross Memorial Hospital in Taplow, Berkshire, and subsequently at Northwick Park Hospital in Harrow. She developed effective drug treatment, and the use of light night splints, together with physiotherapy and exercise routines to prevent deformity in the children's joints and to keep them moving. Most grew to almost normal heights with little residual damage to their joints after the disease burnt itself out. Until her work children had been put in plaster and subjected to bed rest most of the time, thus almost certainly ensuring that they became disabled.

Gout, another rheumatic disease, became controllable, effectively cured, through treatment by drugs like Allopurinol. Osteoarthritis, which it is now known is caused not just by a wearing away of the cartilage in the joints with age but by a disease process remains stubbornly resistant to research, and is still causing a great deal of impairment. Even here, however, salvage methods like joint replacement have done much to overcome disability. In this area, the pioneer was again British – John Charnley who developed the first effective hip replacement technique at the Manchester Royal Infirmary in 1970. There had been attempts earlier in the century and in the 'thirties, particularly by French surgeons, to develop a joint but they failed because they underestimated the tremendous weight, stresses and strains put on joints by quite ordinary human activities, even just walking. Some 40,000 hip replacement operations a year are now performed in Britain. Man-made alternatives have also been developed for many other joints – knees, fingers, wrists, ankles and even the jaw.

Kidney, heart, liver, and lung diseases have also benefited from salvage processes. All can now be replaced, but, unlike in the case of arthritis where artificial prosthesis can be used, this area suffers because there is a shortage of donor organs. Cochlea implants have proved helpful for deaf children and adults.

The treatment of diabetes has provided one of the best of all examples of salvage mechanism: the injection of insulin. Previously people suffered severe disability and invariably died from this condition in which the body fails to deal with glucose. Today there is a growing number of people with both diagnosed and undiagnosed diabetes, mainly because of unhealthy diets leading to obesity. The problem was identified long ago by the Ancient Greeks who gave it the name diabetes, Greek for a siphon. The Persian Ibn Sina, or Avicenna (980-1037) first noted that people suffering from this condition had sweet urine. This led British anatomist Thomas Willis (1621-75) to add mellitis or 'honey sweet' to the description of the disease. Richard Bright (1789-1858) first suggested that the pancreas may have something to do with the complaint. Paul Langerhans (1847-88) identified the cells in the pancreas thought to be responsible for sugar regulation, now known as Islets of Langerhans, but it was experiments by Oskar Minowski and Joseph von Mering in the later half of the nineteenth century which showed beyond doubt that pancreas malfunction was the cause. It was, finally, a British scientist Edward Sharpey-Schafer (1850-1935) who proved that the substance responsible for dealing with carbohydrates was produced by the Islets of Langerhans in the pancreas. He called it insuline, after the Latin for island, insula. Isolation of the insulin was achieved in 1921 by Canadian scientists Fred Banting (1891-1941) and Charles Best (1899-1978). They first injected it into a diabetic dog dying from the condition, and witnessed its revival. The following year, after trying the treatment in many more animals, they injected insulin into a four-year-old dying boy. Of course, he recovered but from then on was dependent on insulin to keep him alive. Literally millions of people are now being saved from death and disability because of the discovery of the pancreatic process involved and the subsequent discovery of insulin.

However, this is not the end of the story since although diabetes is kept at bay by insulin, the disease often results in serious problems for sufferers in terms of heart and kidney disease, strokes, sight impairment and wound care. The new statins are helping to stabilise heart and stroke problems, and there is a growing realisation that early diagnosis and treatment can prevent the eye and kidney complications. Much more work is also being done to improve the delivery of insulin into the patient, and to bring down obesity, one of the major causes of diabetes.

Advances in technology have played a part in overcoming some disability and some diseases: diagnostic tools like Magnetic Resonance Imaging, endoscopes, CAT, PET and MR scans, ultrasound, lasers and tracers have proved of tremendous benefit. Despite progress against disease and causes of disability, nature continues to warn that the battle may be never ending. The classic example is AIDS which appeared to present itself without warning. There have been many theories about from whence it came, few of them convincing. It was in 1981 that the Centers for Disease Control in the United States reported that five men in San Francisco were suffering from a rare type of pneumonia known as pneumocystis carinii, previously found only in people whose immune system had been seriously weakened, usually after the use of drugs to suppress the body's defence mechanism to prevent rejection after having a kidney or other organ transplanted. All five men were homosexuals. The revelation encouraged other doctors in New York and Los Angeles to offer information about disorders in homosexual men they were treating, which seemed to be associated with a breakdown of the immune system. At that time it was labelled as the Gay-Related Immune Disease, but it soon became apparent that this was far from accurate as cases were identified among intravenous drug users, those who had had blood transfusions, particularly haemophiliacs, and heterosexuals of both sexes. Investigations by a Frenchman, Luc Montagnier, demonstrated that a virus which attacked the body's white blood cells – those which defend against disease – was involved, and he named this the Human Immuno-deficiency Virus, or HIV. A test was developed to detect the presence of this virus in the blood so that diagnosis could take place long before the symptoms of AIDS appeared.

Although some treatments have been devised, there is no cure on the horizon. The problem is that HIV mutates, or changes, so fast it is difficult to produce a vaccine. At the same time, treatments for infectious diseases invariably rely on the body's own defence system to support it, and this, of course, is the very system that HIV attacks.

There are also now many instances in which improving medical techniques and better treatment are leading to increases in the number of disabled people needing care and attention. A classic example is traumatic brain injury. In the 1970s and previously, over 90% of the 100,000 people in Britain who suffered serious head injuries in road accidents, falls and assaults would have died. Thankfully today, due to improved surgical and other medical advances, the statistics have reversed, with 90% of them surviving, but many are left with residual problems which need to be addressed before they can be rehabilitated back into society and employment. New charitable enterprises, like Rehab UK, Head Injury Trust and Headway, have emerged to meet their needs as their numbers grow year on year, but with very little recognition from Government that they are aware of the time bomb which is ticking away beneath them.

As would be expected, man continues to try to make advances against these apparently insoluble roots of human impairment. In the vexed field of genetics, genetic engineering and screening beckon enticingly, but with much controversy, to the road of the universal panacea which, it is said, will one day lead to overcoming all sickness and deformity.

Chapter Three

Public Health Measures Against Disease and Disability

The period beginning around the start of the nineteenth century marks a turning point in disability and socio-medical history. In the course of the eighteenth century the population in England and Wales rose from five-and-a-half to nine million. This was due to both a fall in the death rate and a rise in the birth rate, attributed to the establishment of lying-in hospitals, foundling hospitals, general hospitals, better hygiene, improved midwifery and advances in preventive medicine. There was still no established science of epidemiology, community medicine, or population statistics. One of the earliest works on statistics was the *Essay on the Principle of Population* by an English clergyman, Thomas Robert Malthus (1766-1834). In this he showed that the food supply and birth rate increased in arithmetical and geometrical ratio respectively so that poverty is the natural result of increased population. The collection of national statistics really began with the General Register in Somerset House in 1839. The founder of medical statistics is said to have been the Frenchman Armand Trousseau who was the first to apply numerical methods to clinical medicine, and who made statistical studies of typhoid, yellow fever, phthisis, and diphtheria. Through his methods, he was able to show, for instance, that blood letting, the traditional treatment for pneumonia, was of little value. Although his methods took many years to be recognised in his native country, fortunately he found disciples in Britain, where universities established schools of hygiene and medical statistics, and epidemiologists began to study disease in the community.

This is not to say that all was well; far from it. The Industrial Revolution left Britain without any effective system of local Government in the towns that sprang up in its wake. There was overcrowding, grime and filth, cholera and typhus, disabling factors which cried out to be controlled through slum clearance, town planning, and good sewage disposal. In particular, rickets, the crippling bone disease in children, was widespread mainly due to poor nutrition, (lack of vitamin D). Tuberculosis, or consumption as it was then called, also spread rapidly in poor social conditions, and was estimated to kill a quarter of the urban population in Britain. Diphtheria and scarlet fever were other major causes of death among the youngest. At the same time, thousands of chimneys, industrial and domestic, covered everything and everybody in dust and dirt. Cholera known in India and Asia for hundreds of years, reached England in 1831 and, encouraged by the unhygienic conditions in the rapidly expanding industrial towns, spread mercilessly from contaminated drinking water.

In the face of this onslaught, the first successful campaign for public health and hygiene began in 1838 led by Sir Edwin Chadwick. He was helped considerably by the earlier work of William Farr, abstract compiler at the Registrar General's Department, who came up with the first national disease classification. These life-tables, as he called them, enabled Farr to show how the census and mortality records could be used to detect public illnesses and disabilities. They indicated how life expectation at different ages varied according to where people lived, their occupations, wealth and hygiene. As Secretary to the Poor Law Commission, he first tried to cut the cost of poverty to the community by a new Poor Law in 1834. This made conditions in workhouses harsh and uncomfortable on the grounds that it would make them cheaper to run, deter dependency, and return people to the workplace quicker. His theory failed: more paupers turned up at workhouse doors than before. Thankfully Chadwick then concluded that most poverty was not caused by fecklessness but by disease, and at last observed that many of those in workhouses were sick and disabled.

This drew him to Farr's life-tables, and consequently to ways of reforming public hygiene. He looked into most of the social elements of urban life – sewers, water supplies, open spaces, burial grounds, and slums. It was a report published by the Poor Law Commission which gave Chadwick the spur for reform. This reported that sickness and epidemics, caused by a lack of good sanitation, put a great strain on the local rates. There was also much evidence in the report about the shocking slums in the East End of London, which added to the rapid spread of disease once it had begun. Chadwick engineered the placing of a question in the House of Lords, part of which was a request to make a similar enquiry for the whole of England. This was granted, and Chadwick undertook the survey. In 1842 the Poor Law Commission brought out his celebrated *Report on the Sanitary Conditions of the Labouring Population of Great Britain*.

This concluded that insanitary living conditions and filth accounted for the poor health and shortened life spans of the poor. The comparisons were startling and odious: in London's Bethnal Green, for instance, the average age at death of a labourer was sixteen, whereas among the well-to-do it was forty-five. The report was damning, and written in the language of the reformer:

> '...Whilst the houses, streets, courts, lanes and streams are polluted and rendered pestilential, the civic officers have generally contented themselves with the most barbarous expedients, or sit still amidst the pollution, with the resignation of Turkish fatalists, under the supposed destiny of the prevalent ignorance, sloth and filth. The whole family of the labouring man in the manufacturing towns rise early, before daylight in winter-time, to go to their work; they toil hard, and they return to their houses late at night. It is a serious consequence, as well as discomfort to them to have to fetch water at a distance out of doors from the pump or river on every occasion that it may

be wanted, whether it may be in cold, in rain, or in snow. The minor comforts of cleanliness are, of course, forgone, to avoid the immediate and greater discomfort of having to fetch water. It is only when the infant enters upon breathing existence, and when the man has ceased to breathe – at the moment of birth and at the hour of death – that he is really well washed.'

In all major towns, the report concluded, pauperism was largely due to fever from overcrowding, bad waste disposal, dirty water and poor diet. The report advocated improving drainage, water supply and the removal of all refuse from houses, streets and roads.

It was difficult to ignore such fervour and condemnation. Chadwick then led an ambitious campaign to improve town life for the poor. He urged that a national public health authority be established with the responsibility of directing local health boards to provide drainage, street cleansing and paving, clean drinking water, and sanitary regulations of dwellings. A Royal Commission on the Health of Towns sat between 1843 and 1845, which largely backed Chadwick's recommendations. The result was the first Public Health Act, passed in 1848, which created a central authority, the General Board of Health. The provisions of the Act could be imposed by the Board on any local authority with an annual death rate of 23 per thousand or over, or by means of a tenth of the ratepayers petitioning it. Either way, the local council was then forced to set up a local board of health, which then took action to improve drainage, sanitary inspection, water and gas supplies, and to pay for this by raising local rates. Perhaps most important of all, they had to appoint Medical Officers of Health whose job it was to remove all environmental hazards. By 1853, one hundred and three towns had adopted the Act. Chadwick and the Board were far from popular: local councils refused, as they put it, to be bullied into health. This unpopularity led to the Board's demise in 1854, and a new body was formed on a medical model of public health. John Simon was appointed as Britain's first chief medical administrator at the new Medical Department of the Privy Council. His chief tactic was to produce a succession of reports on scientific investigations of poor housing conditions and industrial dangers. A string of legislative measures followed which gave local authorities more powers on matters such as polluted rivers, refuse, industrial waste and smoke, clean water supplies, housing, vaccination, and compulsory purchase for sanitary purposes. The Public Health Act 1875 made it mandatory to appoint a Medical Officer of Health in every sanitary district in England and Wales. Thus public health in Britain had made a transition from social action by individuals to an established medical specialty.

Linked with this progress was the issue of compulsory health measures. This was particularly exemplified by an Act in 1853 which made vaccination against smallpox mandatory. This may have been for the public good, but it was unpopular. An anti-vaccination campaign started and continued for decades. In 1874 the National Anti-Compulsory Vaccination League was formed, and then in 1880 the London Society for the Abolition of Compulsory Vaccination. The campaigning must have had some effect, for in 1909 Parliament decided to do away with compulsory vaccination. Another target was sexually transmitted diseases, with compulsory measures being introduced after high levels were diagnosed in the armed forces. The Contagious Diseases Act (1864) made it possible to force women suspected of prostitution in some localities, like those around ports and bases, to undergo medical examinations. If they were found to be infected they could be compulsorily detained for up to three months for treatment. Further legislation later extended regular inspection to known prostitutes. These measures, often used inappropriately by the authorities, engendered opposition from women's activists and were repealed.

The compulsory notification of other communicable diseases empowered medical officers of health to quarantine people with specific contagious or infectious diseases, among them smallpox and tuberculosis. Rich TB sufferers had already found the benefit of entering sanatoria high in the mountains or in warm climates. At the end of the century people began to ask why the poor were not offered the same fresh air opportunities to help with their disease. So much so that by 1910 forty-one public sanitoria had been specially built in Britain, and under the National Insurance Act (1911) financial support was afforded to the families of the people who entered them. Fresh air was seen as paramount in treating the disease, though some patients complained that this could be too much of a good thing. Windows were always open, even in the depth of winter, and it was not unknown for beds to be wheeled into the open with snow and frost about.

Public health measures did not stop with the close of the nineteenth century. Perhaps the most famous measures of the twentieth century were those dealing with air quality, particularly those which insisted on individuals and industries burning smokeless fuel. Even if that menace has been largely replaced by fumes from cars, The Clean Air Act did at least put a stop to the famous pea-souper fogs which killed huge numbers of people. There is little doubt that public health measures like slum clearance, clean water, efficient sewage disposal, and general cleanliness, did improve health and prevent disability. The drop in Britain of diseases like typhus, infectious diseases, tuberculosis, whooping cough, scarlet fever, and rheumatic fever, was dramatic. The rise in population in the late nineteenth and twentieth centuries is largely due to these factors and better nutrition, with public health measures undoubtedly making the greater contribution.

Chapter Four

Disability and the Workplace

From the earliest times there has always been illness, injury and
disability associated with the workplace. Yet, in effect, the seeds of
occupational medicine were not sown until the turn of the eighteenth century through the work of the Italian Bernardo
Ramazzini, known as the father of occupational medicine, from
1682 until his death in 1714 Professor of Medical Theory at
Modena. His first epidemiological work discussed outbreaks of
malaria associated with heavy rain and flooding, but his chief
concern was the collection throughout many years of observations among workers in over fifty trades. These drew attention to
diseases and disabilities resulting from bad working postures and
mercury poisoning. The result was his *'On Diseases of Workers'*
which appeared in 1700. In truth, of course, diseases of the
workplace have existed since man began to have collective aims
and ambitions. The ancient Egyptians, in their never ending
search for gold, worked prisoners, and the children of prisoners,
in their gold mines until they became disabled in lung, joint and
limb and finally died of exhaustion. In ancient Greece, the 'mechanical arts' and those who performed them were stigmatised.
Xenophon in his *Oeconomicus* reports Socrates as saying: 'What
are called the mechanical arts carry a social stigma and are rightly
dishonoured in our cities. For these arts damage the bodies of
those who work at them or who have charge of them, by com-

pelling the workers to a sedentary life and to an indoor life, by compelling them, indeed, in some cases to spend the whole day by the fire. This physical degeneration results also in deterioration of the soul…'

It is not surprising , this being the attitude, that the workers were looked down upon and scant attention was paid to their health and welfare. The possibility that workplace factors could have any relevance to disability was ignored for centuries, though it now appears so obvious, because nobody cared. It was Ramazzini who first advised doctors when making a diagnosis to ask a patient to describe his occupation. However, even he had a small foundation to build upon. Georg Bauer, born at Glauchau in Saxony, and known more commonly as Georgius Agricola, published his *De Re Meallica* in 1556 in which he described in twelve volumes every aspect of mining. The final volume recorded accounts of the diseases and accidents which caused disability among the miners, including the ill-effects of poor ventilation. His were the first descriptions of the harmful effects of dust inhalation, and of a disability of the lung which seemed to be associated with this, causing progressive emaciation: '…the dust which is stirred and beaten up by digging, penetrates into the windpipe and lungs and produces difficulty in breathing and the disease which the Greeks called asthma. If the dust has corrosive qualities, it eats away the lungs, and implants consumption in the body. In the mines of the Carpathian Mountains, women are found who have married seven husbands, all of whom this terrible consumption has carried off to a premature death.'

To his credit, Agricola advocated that miners should wear veils to keep at least some of the dust out of their lungs. Eleven years after Agricola's books appeared, came what was the first monograph devoted entirely to the diseases of mine and smelter workers. Strangely, it was published 26 years after the death of its author, Aureolus Theophrastus Bombastus, thankfully known usually as Paracelsus. He believed and wrote that the lung sickness came 'through the power of the stars, in that their peculiar characters are boiled out, which settle on the lungs in three different ways: in a mercurial manner like a sublimated smoke that coagulates, like a salt spirit, which passes from resolution to coagulation, and thirdly, like a sulphur, which is precipitated on the walls by roasting'.

It was Ramazzini, however, with his passionate commitment to eradicate disease from the workplace, who made the first real impact in convincing employers and doctors that there was a link between work and disability and that it should concern them: 'Medicine, like jurisprudence', he stated, 'should make a contribution to the well-being of workers and see to it that, so far as possible, they should exercise their callings without harm. So I for my part have done what I could and have not thought it unbecoming to make my way into the lowliest workshops and study the mysteries of the mechanical arts.'

Although he was wrong in a great many assumptions, he was far ahead of his time on many matters relating to workers' welfare. He advocated rest and intervals in work. He wrote at length about the need for change of posture and exercise. He condemned lack of ventilation, and said that workers in dusty trades should work in spacious surroundings, wash their faces, rinse out their mouths with water, and give up work immediately symptoms of breathing disorders indicated that the lungs were threatened.

It was some decades later that occupational medicine was born. It was conceived in Britain, and not before time. The early industrial revolution tore through society, leaving gaping wounds in those who provided it with labour. Small children and women were particularly at risk because they provided the cheapest of cheap labour. The basis of this maltreatment of children was the 1563 Statute of Artificers which created the apprenticeship system. Initially this meant that the apprentice was given board and lodging in his master's house. In return he would be taught a trade, but the rules were harsh and heavily weighted towards the employer. In effect, the system afforded an endless source of unpaid labour, with the apprentice bound, some said enslaved, for a long period. One particularly bad example of the system was the plight of the Climbing Boys. In the seventeenth century, after the Great Fire of London in 1666, long, narrow and tortuous chimneys became fashionable, and as a consequence chimney sweeps were in demand. Their design made the chimneys difficult to sweep and use of boys to climb through them, dislodging the soot as they went, became widespread. These unfortunates had to be particularly tiny to squeeze through flues only seven inches wide, and they were often sold into apprenticeship by their parents for a few pounds. Their reluctance to climb swiftly into the filth and darkness above them was frequently overcome by lighting straw fires beneath them. Some were suffocated, many suffered diseases of the lungs. A surgeon named Percival Potts (1714-88) also found a link between scrotal cancer and the soot to which the boys were exposed. At night their masters usually kept them in cellars so that they could not escape, with a bag of soot for a mattress and another as a blanket.

William Blakes's *Songs of Innocence* was published in 1789 and the first verse sets the scene:

When my mother died I was very young,
And my father sold me while yet my tongue
Could scarcely cry 'weep! 'weep! 'weep!
So your chimney I sweep, and in soot I sleep.

Despite the fact that an Act passed in 1814 forbade the use of boys for sweeping chimneys, nobody was named to enforce it. The practice continued and the numbers of boys used actually increased. Dickens, in *Oliver Twist* (1837), and Charles Kingsley (1863), in *The Water Babies*, both wrote of the sad lives of the climbing boys. It was not until 1875, when Lord Shaftesbury produced an Act which made it the responsibility of the police to issue a yearly licence to chimney sweeps, and to ensure that children were not being used before issuing it, that the children ceased to be employed as tiny, helpless, human brushes.

Friedrich Engels, (1820-1895) among many observations of working conditions as a whole, made particular reference to those endured by children in glass making factories:

> '...the hard labour, the irregularity of the hours, the frequent
> night work, and especially the great heat of the working place,
> engender in children general debility and disease, stunted
> growth, and especially infections of the eye, bowel complaints,
> and rheumatic and bronchial infections. Many of the children
> are pale, have red eyes, often blind for weeks at a time, suffer
> from violent nausea, vomiting, coughs, colds and rheuma-
> tism...The glass-blowers usually die young of debility or chest
> infections.'

Overall, in British trade and industry, apprenticeship became
the lot of the poorest, particularly the 'poor law', or parish,
children. The child who became ill or disabled was quickly
discarded into the workhouse. Although the apprenticeship
clauses of the 1563 Statue of Artificers were repealed in 1814,
these did not apply to the poor parish apprentices who continued
to be sold into comparative slavery until 1844.

The apprenticeship system went into decay as the industrial
revolution developed, but parish apprentices were still a strong
source of factory fodder, and other working children were totally
unprotected. The system left employers with a belief that children
could be worked long and hard for very little reward. In the new
factories, like the mills, it was commonplace to work children for
up to eighteen hours a day. At the same time women were enticed
into the factories by the fact that very little work was available
elsewhere at the rates, to women at least, being paid by the mill
owners.

There were many dubious practices. Labour agents or con-
tractors took children from the workhouses and the poorest
families of the cities and sold them for a fiver a time to the mill
and factory owners. Other children, from the countryside around
new industrial towns, were driven into the factories by the
poverty of their parents, and they often became the only source
of family income. In '*A Memoir of Robert Blincoe, a Poor Orphan
Boy, sent from the Workhouse of St.Pancras in London at Seven
Years of Age to Endure the horrors of a Cotton Mill through his*

Infancy and Youth with a minute detail of his Sufferings, Being the First Memoir of the Kind Published, which appeared in 1832, came the first published details of the cruelty to children and the stress and disability caused to them. It described the use of the strap to make them work faster, and having to compete with pigs for the scraps to overcome hunger. The children's staple diet was 'water porridge' and oaten cake. Frances Trollope, the mother of the famous Anthony, followed this in 1840 with the harrowing story of *'The Life and Adventures of Michael Armstrong, the Factory Boy'*.

The book by Blincoe described the disabling cruelties of the boys' treatment:

'Long before one wound had healed, similar acts of cruelty produced others, so that on many occasions his head was excoriated and bruised to a degree that rendered him offensive to himself and others, and so intolerably painful as to deprive him of rest at night however weary he might be. In consequence of such wounds his head was overrun by vermin. Being reduced to this deplorable state, some brute of a quack doctor used to apply a pitch cap or plaster to his head. After it had been given time, and when its adhesion was supposed to be complete, the terrible doctor used to lay forcibly hold of one corner and tear the whole scalp from his head at once. This was the common remedy; I should not exaggerate the agonies it occasioned were I to affirm that it must be equal to anything inflicted by the American savages on helpless prisoners with their scalping knives and tomahawks.'

Such cruelty and exploitation had been in place for a long time, with not unexpected accompanying ill health and disability. The hovels in which many of the child workers lived were overcrowded and often dirty. There were frequent outbreaks of 'factory fever', a polite name for typhus. One such outbreak, in 1784 in the Radcliffe Mills, Manchester, led to the beginnings of conscience and social reform. The mills belonged to none other than the family of Sir Robert Peel, at that time Home Secretary, who was so appalled at the consequences of the conditions in his own mills that he took up the cause of factory children and became known as the father of industrial legislation. At the same time, an enquiry by Manchester magistrates undertaken by Dr Thomas Percival into the typhus outbreak came to the conclusion that it was 'supported, diffused and aggravated by the ready communication of contagion to numbers crowded together… and by the injury done to young persons through confinement and too-long-continued labour; to which several evils the cotton mills have given occasion'.

The enquiry report advocated shorter hours and no night work, and that the children be given the opportunity to learn and to play games. Later Dr Percival formed the Manchester Board of Health which voluntarily supervised working conditions in the mills in Manchester. The impact of this helped Peel's parliamentary efforts and his success with his Health and Morals of Apprentices Act 1802. Under this, hours for apprentices were fixed at twelve a day, with no night work, it became mandatory for the walls of factories to be washed down at least twice a year, and a system of inspection by volunteer clergymen and others was set up.

Unfortunately, Peel's Act did not protect the parish apprentices and children who were employed but who were not under apprenticeships, and they continued to be cruelly exploited. Sadly, too, the appointment of inspectors was rarely made or taken up. There were still some 20,000 children employed in mills in 1802. In 1816 Parliament passed an Act which made it illegal to send parish apprentices further than forty miles from their own parish. In the same year the first Parliamentary Commission to look into child labour was established, with Sir Robert Peel as its Chairman. Peel recognised that there was now a need to protect children who were not apprentices:

'I most anxiously press upon the committee that unless some parliamentary interference takes place, the benefits of the Apprentice Bill will be entirely lost,' he told the Committee, 'the practice of employing parish apprentices will cease, their place will be wholly supplied by other children, between whom and their masters no permanent contract is likely to exist, and for whose good treatment there will not be the slightest security...Gentlemen, if parish apprentices were formerly deemed worthy of the care of Parliament, I trust you will not withhold from the unprotected children of the present day an equal measure of mercy, as they have no masters who are obliged to support them in sickness or during unfavourable periods of trade.'

The Factory Act 1819 which resulted from Peel's Parliamentary Committee was a disappointment. Few changes were made in children's working conditions, apart from making nine the minimum age of their employment and limiting hours, but, importantly, it did establish the principle of extending the law to workers other than bound apprentices. Reformers like Robert Owen and Jeremy Bentham fought campaigns for better health and education among factory workers. Having first tried to improve conditions at a mill he owned in Manchester, Owen's main reforms were made at his New Lanark mills. Among the 2000 employees he inherited from the previous owner were 500 children, most of them acquired aged five or six from the poor houses of Edinburgh and Glasgow. He found, too, that housing conditions, sanitation and education were intolerable. Owen set out to improve his workers' lot through his principles of educational philanthropy, principles he published in 1813 in 'A New View of Society, or Essays on the Principle of the Formation of the Human Character'. Over the 28 years from 1800 when he acquired the New Lanark mills he abolished the employment of very young children, improved training amongst all workers, provided unemployment pay, built new housing and methods of sanitation, and founded schools. He became the first employer in Britain to start infant schools for children who came into his mills, and they were taught English and arithmetic, as well as nature study, singing and dancing. The results were impressive, the children produced by the system being completely different from the unfortunates who had, literally, gone through the mill before. Owen was much lauded in the press, both in Britain and internationally, and received famous visitors at his mills.

He then advocated setting up communities of 1200 people in which families had charge of their children until the age of three, but then the community brought them up. It is not surprising that most other factory owners were not impressed. They found ways to discredit him through his hostility to the Church. By that time Owen had founded four communities – in England, Scotland, Ireland and the United States – but these had to be wound up and Owen lost almost all his fortune.

On the whole most factory owners still believed that trade and profit were all that mattered, and as new machinery became available forced wages lower on the excuse that labour was less and less needed. This attitude produced a climate of social discontent, not surprisingly much of it connected with terrible working conditions. The Luddite Movement, named after Ned Ludd, a possibly mythical Sherwood Forest leader, was a protest against the inhumane pressure brought by new machinery and harsh employers. Its first focus was the framework knitters in Nottingham who were being exploited and made even more impoverished by new methods of production so that their wages went down whilst production went up. Between 1811 and 1816 the Luddites took out their frustration on machinery not only in Nottingham but in Lancashire. For their trouble some were hanged and others were sent into exile in Australia.

Many workers believed that the only avenue of change was through Parliament, and established the Reform Movement. Great meetings were organised. One of these, held in St.Peter's Field, Manchester in 1819, has become infamous as the Peterloo Massacre. Sixty thousand people gathered to hear the radical orator James Leigh Hunt. The meeting was declared illegal and the Yeomanry arrived to arrest the speaker. Although no resistance was given, they charged their way through the crowd, killing eleven people, and injuring some four hundred others through sword wounds and trampling. The discontent was not all in factories: in the winter of 1830-31, farm workers in the south protested and demonstrated against low wages, brought about, they judged, by the introduction of new threshing machines. Three of the leaders went to the gallows and 420 to penal colonies in Australia. Powerful employers resisted the reform of working conditions. In Victorian times, too, many people had the attitude of Mr.Scrooge in Dickens' *Christmas Carol:* 'What then, if he be like to die, he had better do it, and decrease the surplus population'. The Chartist movement, over a 12 year period starting in 1834, sought better factory conditions and wages, and also produced the People's Charter which demanded electoral and parliamentary reform. Despite obtaining hundreds of thousands of signatures on a petition, the Government rejected demands for reform, and slowly, despite riots and strikes, the movement lost impetus and died.

Against this background there were some attempts at reform in the factories, largely by enlightened individuals and some of the first trades unions. Most of the workplace laws related to the protection of children, but the Act of 1833 did have wider implications because it enforced the appointment of factory inspectors. One of the first four inspectors was Robert Baker, a Leeds surgeon, who three years earlier had advised a factory owner who was worried that children were being disabled by their hours and conditions of work to appoint a medical officer to observe the effects of work on the childen's health.

The rapid pace of the industrial revolution had resulted in an inevitable conflict between 'capital', factory owners anxious to get the most out of their investments, and 'labour', workers anxious to try to protect themselves and to get a fair return for their contribution to the wealth they helped to create.

The first trade unions were local bodies, more like friendly societies who helped their members. However, they received a setback at the turn of the nineteenth century when uprisings among peasants in France caused fears in Britain and resulted in the Combination Acts of 1799 and 1800. These were aimed at trade unions since it was believed their meetings provided opportunities for treasonable developments. Trade unions remained illegal from 1799 until 1825, when the combination laws were repealed. Fortunately, the enforced 'rest' appeared to do some trade unions good, for they emerged stronger than ever and many, with the development of nationwide industries like the railways, became national bodies. The National Association of United Trades for the Protection of Labour was founded in 1845, but failed to find strong support from trade unions who were still, understandably, obsessed with putting matters right in their own industries. The first embryonic trades union congress met in Manchester in 1868, representing over a hundred thousand trade unionists. Although most of them concentrated on collective bargaining, insurance, and social benefits for sick and disabled members, working conditions and occupational health hazards were not neglected.

Among individuals who cared enough about workers to attempt their own reforms, perhaps the most outstanding was Samuel Greg, who lived between 1758 and 1834. He built Quarry Bank, a spinning mill in the village of Styal, and around it a model village with school, church, houses for workers and a home for apprentices. In 1789 a physician was appointed at £10 a year to serve Quarry Bank mill. In 1795 Dr Peter Holland was being paid £12 per annum to take good medical care of the apprentices. His diaries of the daily treatments given became the first record of a medical service in industry. These were the beginnings of occupational medicine. As yet, though, there had been no systematic recording of the disease and disability brought about by long hours in the British workplace. It was a doctor named Charles Turner Thackray, born in Yorkshire in 1795, who decided it should be his role to correct this deficiency, and published in 1830 his '*The Effects of the Principal Arts, Trades and Professions, and of Civic States and Habits of Living, on Health and Longevity, with Suggestions for the Removal of many of the Agents which produce Disease and shorten the Duration of Life*'. Thackray's zeal shone through in the introduction to his book: 'Most persons, who reflect on the subject, will be inclined to admit that our employments are in a considerable degree injurious to health: but they believe, or profess to believe, that the evils cannot be counteracted, and urge that an investigation of such evils can produce only pain and discontent. From a reference to fact and observation I reply, that in many of our occupations, the injurious agents might be immediately removed or diminished. Evils are suffered to exist, even when the means of correction are known and easily applied. Thoughtlessness or apathy is the only obstacle to success.'

In general terms, Thackray first underlined the fact that bad occupational postures caused disabilities, and, secondly, pinpointed the disability caused to children. Although there had been some improvement, many thousands of children were still becoming avoidably disabled in mills and other factories. At the time Thackray made his study: 'Children from seven to fifteen years of age go to work at half-past five in the morning, and leave at seven in the evening…and thus spend twelve hours a day, for five or six years, in an atmosphere of flax dust. Serious injury from such employment we should expect at any age, but especially during the period of growth.'

Thackray noted disabilities and deformities found especially among weavers, burlers, clothdrawers, and tailors. Their spines were generally curved, and added to this pulmonary consumption, caused by dust, was usually an added burden. Dust of all kinds became a particular target. He found it caused problems for miners, noting that the dust meant that they seldom reached the age of forty, and also for knife grinders in Sheffield, who, because they inhaled dust from a dry grindstone, generally died between the ages of twenty-eight and thirty-two. He recognised the link between dust inhalation and tuberculosis, and recommended that it could be tackled by introducing better ventilation and protective mouthpieces. In all he looked at some 120 occupations in and around Leeds where he lived and worked. He detected the disabling effects of lead poisoning, which caused great pain and disability, and ultimately lead to palsy in house painters and potters making glazed ware. Thackray worked out that it would cost but a halfpenny more to make a glazed pot if lead were not used.

Unfortunately Thackray himself died of tuberculosis at the age of thirty-seven in 1833, but his pioneering work left a rich legacy to enable reformers to make their cases to, and often within, Parliament. Sir John Simon, the first Chief Medical Officer to the Local Government Board, acknowledged Britain's debt to Thackray more than fifty years later: 'By his eminently trustworthy book, he made it a matter of common knowledge, and of State responsibility, that, with certain of our chief industries, special influences, often of an evidently removable kind, are apt to be associated, which, if permitted to remain, give painful disease and premature disablement and death to the employed persons.'

Thackray's early death was a blow to occupational medicine, but the climate his book created helped produce the evidence for legislation, enacted in 1844, giving factory inspectors the power to appoint a doctor in each district to examine young people working in factories. It also drew attention to the working conditions in the mining industry, where children five, six and seven were still being employed. Because they were a cheaper form of locomotion than horses, these unfortunates were harnessed to trucks of coal down in the mines which, because of lack of headroom, they pulled as they moved on all-fours, resulting in disability and disease. Women were equally maltreated as a source of cheap labour. In the face of this Lord Shaftsbury appointed in 1840 a Royal Commission on the employment of children in mines. Its report was so damning, leaving many MPs in tears when it was presented to the House, that it led to the passing of the Mines Act 1842. This established the principle of Government inspection in the conduct of the industry, and was followed by seven Mines Regulation Acts over the next half century dealing with health and safety.

From the middle of the nineteenth century occupational medicine became so recognised that the Factory Acts were extended to take in unhealthy working conditions in all workplaces, and legislation was also directed against specific disease causative agents. Mines and mills had been the target of earlier legislation, but in many other industries health and safety remained unregulated. Dreadful conditions still remained in the potteries, paper making, print, steel and many other industries. A series of reports was issued between 1863 and 1867 on lucifer match making, paper staining, china making and cutlery manufacture. The manufacturing processes in all these trades resulted in disability and disfigurement to workers, but employers were reluctant to initiate reform themselves. The match trade was notorious because it caused pain and ugly phosphorus necrosis or 'phossy jaw.' The affliction attacked young girls and women almost exclusively employed in the making of matches. The manufacture of paper and textiles at that time used green arsenites of copper mixed with arsenic, causing illness and incapacity. Both Sheffield cutlery grinders and glazers in the pottery industries were prone to asthma and consumption because of the dust their working methods produced. The report led to the Factories and Workshops Act 1867 under which unregulated industries like these were brought under control. It was the Factories (Prevention of Lead Poisoning) Act 1883 which became the very first Act of Parliament to regulate against a specific occupational hazard, and was the forerunner of the present system of prescribed diseases from which to protect employees in all trades.

It was a system much needed in the twentieth century, as it is still in the twenty-first, with the rapid increase in scientific knowledge in the manufacturing processes, particularly in the chemical industry. The idea of prevention had been introduced by the pioneers of occupational medicine, but it was not until well into the twentieth century that the concept of compensation was introduced. Compensation for occupational accidents became part of the legislation with the Workmen's Compensation Act 1897, but diseases were not part of this until a 1906 Act, which included anthrax; also lead, mercury, phosphorus, and arsenic poisoning, together with a description of the processes to disease and disability. From then on, under subsequent Acts, other occupational diseases were added. They produced some strange language: telegraphist's cramp in 1908, dope poisoning in 1918, twister's cramp in 1921, skin damage due to X-rays and manganese poisoning in 1924, and mule spinner's cancer in 1932.

By 1945, forty-one diseases were covered. There was an addition to the legislation in 1986 with the Social Security (Prescribed Diseases) Regulations which provided a list of prescribed diseases and the occupations relating to which they are prescribed. The associated 'Reporting of Industrial Diseases and Dangerous Occurrences Regulations' came into force at the same time.

Although Britain has led the way in occupational health, largely due to the industrial revolution having started here, there were developments and progress elsewhere. In 1906, the Permanent Commission for the Study of Industrial Disease was established by Luigi Devoto of Milan. This became the International Commission on Occupational Health, which established many committees covering many specific areas of occupational health and prevention.

The International Labour Organisation (ILO) has also made a significant contribution, not surprisingly since one of its mandates on its creation under the Treaty of Versailles was 'the protection of the worker against sickness or disease arising out of his employment'. Shortly after its foundation the ILO formed an industrial hygiene section, which first produced an Encyclopedia of Occupational Health and Safety, and has over the years made recommendations on numerous specific health and safety matters. At its conventions over the years numerous recommendations have been made on occupational health: anthrax protection; lead poisoning (women and children); white phosphorus 1919; white lead (painting) 1921; workmen's compensation (occupational diseases) 1925 and 1934; protection of health workers 1953; occupational health services 1959; radiation protection 1960; employment injury benefits 1964; benzene 1971; prevention and control of occupational cancer 1974; working environment 1977; occupational safety and health 1981; occupational health services 1985; safety in the use of asbestos 1986. Other recommendations cover minimum age, night work, protection of women and young people, medical examinations and the lifting and carrying of heavy weights.

The European Economic Community since its formation has produced measures under the headings of protection against dangerous substances, the prevention of the dangers and harmful effects of machinery, and the monitoring and inspecting of workplace conditions. In the United States occupational health was always the responsibility of the individual states, resulting in patchy protection. Large companies were left to develop their own health policies.

In 1970 Congress put on the statute book the Occupational Safety and Health Administration Act and created a Federal body, the Occupational Safety and Health Administration. Individual States kept their own bodies which work under the Federal organisation.

The medical specialty of occupational health has expanded considerably since those days when Ramazzini noted the disabilities and diseases associated with some early occupations. It is now extremely sophisticated and its province covers diseases associated with chemical agents, aromatic compounds, gases, physical agents, pressure, radiation, inorganic and organic dusts, microbiological agents, occupational cancer and asthma, diseases of the skin, and damage to reproductive health, and physical and mental working practices.

Chapter Five

'Freak' Shows

People with disabilities and deformities have always been the subjects of 'curiosity', jokes and shows. Medieval 'cripples', particularly children, were exploited for amusement. Roman beggars made slaves of crippled children and exhibited their deformities by the roadside. Often children were purposely maimed or their infirmities made greater to increase their 'appeal' and curiosity value. Fiction is full of references to fools, jesters and those with deformities. In the *Hunchback of Notre Dame*, Victor Hugo records that the boy hunchback Quasimodo was found in the year 1466 when he was four-years-old 'upon the bed it was customary to expose foundlings of public charity'. Those that came across the boy expressed the fears and contempt they felt for those with deformities: 'It sees with but one eye; there is a wart over the other.' 'What do you predict from this pretended foundling?' 'I think it would be better for the people of Paris if this sorcerer were laid on a fagot 'a fine flaming fagot.'

Royal courts throughout Europe were entertained by deformed jesters and fools. In Verdi's *Rigoletto*, set in Mantua in the sixteenth century, there is a deformed jester, object of great public fun and amusement. The 18th through to the 20th centuries saw the development of highly organised exploitation of disability, which indeed became an industry. The 'freak' shows came into their own. Some of the earliest records of them are

French. A German without arms and legs who performed at Parisian Fairs beginning in 1716 was able to write, play a drum and make houses out of cards. Another young man, a handsome sixteen-year-old Venetian with hands growing from his shoulders and feet from his haunches, performed body gyrations at the Saint-Laurent fair in 1752. In 1779 at Saint-Germain a Liegois, a schoolmaster who had no arms, was put on show as he uncorked bottles, drank, smoked, tied knots, threaded needles, played cards, and did many other things which showed that being born without upper limbs left him by no means helpless.

Some of the earliest freaks concerned those of widely differing heights. An eight-foot tall giant was displayed at Saint-Germain in 1731. At the other end of the scale midgets were greatly sought after for showing. Perhaps the most famous, some might say in typical French fashion, was the 'Giant Dwarf', who first appeared as a four-year-old child. He was said to be 'formed as fortunately as the most vigorous man beyond the finest proportions in the virile organ, has the diverse abilities of it such as erection, ejaculation'. It was claimed, and shown, that it was at the approach of a woman that his virility manifested itself. Shamelessly his showman verified his age through a record of birth, his teeth and his linguistic ability.

Londoners were as avid as their Parisian counterparts in their interest in freaks. As well as putting them on show in the early 18th century at spectacles such as St.Batholomew's Fair, Britain's earliest showmen exhibited at inns, although at that stage most of the exhibits were said to come from overseas. All could be purchased, as well as looked at, for a price set by the exhibitor. There was 'a young Oronuto savage from Ethiopia', and an 'elephantiasis man covered all over with scales like unto those of a large fish'. There was also 'a healthy Man who is covered all over his body with solid quills, there is likewise a Youth, his son, about seven years of age who is covered all over with solid quills like this father, except his face, the palms of his hands and bottoms of his feet'. Father and son, incidentally, could be purchased for two thousands guineas. There was also the exhibition of a Cherokee chief, dressed only in shirts, trowsers (sic) and mantles. 'The Nobility, Gentry and Curious in General' were also given the opportunity to stare at 'the white negro girl', an albino.

Sometimes lurid advertisements heralded new exhibits or older ones of particular interest. In April 1751 'The Gentleman's Magazine' carried an advertisement for Mr.Mandferdit, a centaur, half man, half horse. 'The hours of showing are from 10 in the morning until 4 in the afternoon, the rest of the time being necessary to comb and curry himself, stir up his litter and study English history'. He was also on offer to be 'let out to great ladies to take the air on'. Unsurprisingly, this was a complete fraud, a sailor whose back end was a stuffed horse.

The amusements increased and became of wider interest. Wordsworth's description of Bartholomew's Fair in '*The Prelude*' summed up the wonder and awe of it all to the people who flocked to ogle:

'Above the press and danger of the crowd
Upon some showman's platform...

All movables of wonder, from all parts,
Are here – Albinos, painted Indians, Dwarfs,
The Horse of knowledge, and the learned Pig,
The Stone-eater, and the man that swallows fire,
Giants, Ventriloquists, the Invisible Girl,
The Bust that speaks and moves its goggling eyes,
The Wax-work, Clock-work, all the marvellous craft
Of modern Merlins, Wild Beasts, Puppet shows,
All out-o'-the-way, far-fetched, perverted things,
All freaks of nature, all Promethean thoughts
Of man, his dullness, madness, and their feats
All jumbled up together, to compose
A Parliament of Monsters'.

The later freak shows have these origins, but they can also be traced, particularly in the United States, to scientists who opened museums as a means of education of the general public, which sometimes also included strange phenomena brought back by sailors and explorers. The pretext for including either pictures or bottled samples of those born with deformities, particularly Siamese twins, was, it was claimed, because they were of scientific interest. Indeed, the Victorians developed the science of teratology, the study of 'monsters', bent on establishing a scientific classification for them. *The Lancet* and *The British Medical Journal* actually addressed the problems of discussing the physical deformities shown in disabled people in ways that would observe Victorian standards. The reason was simple: for almost half of the nineteenth century the Christian churches did not look favourably on the theatre and other amusements, but they fully accepted the benefits of attending lectures, education and science, and anything connected with these edifying pursuits. The museum thus provided an ideal disguise. The very fact that scientists were interested justified, at least in their eyes, the showman in meeting the morbid curiosity of his public. In turn, doctors and scientists often visited freak shows and freaks, and their comments on the nature and origins of these 'creatures' led to even more publicity for them.

In Britain freak shows had become so widespread by the middle of the nineteenth century that the humourous weekly *Punch* noted that 'deformitomania' was a new social disease characterised by almost insatiable fascination with freaks. The magazine noted: 'The walls of the Egyptian Hall in Piccadilly are placarded from top to bottom with bills announcing the exhibition of some frightful object within, and the building itself will soon be known as the Hall of Ugliness. We cannot understand the cause of the now prevailing taste for deformity, which seems to grow by what it feeds upon…We understand that an exhibition consisting of the most frightful objects in nature is about to be formed at the Egyptian Hall under the title of Hideorama. Poor Madame Tussaud, with her Chamber of Horrors, is quite thrown into the shade by the number of real enormities and deformities that are now to be seen, as the showmen say, Alive! alive!'

However, it was the legendary Phineas Taylor Barnum who saw the real possibilities of the freak show, and exploited disabled people unmercilessly. He put together a collection of 'human monsters' – a troupe of giants, dwarfs, fat ladies, thin men, albinos, bearded women, armless and legless wonders, and Siamese, or conjoined, twins. The origins of the Barnum empire began with museums. By the mid 19th century, most cities in the States had museums but these were finding it difficult to keep going. Those few that were on a sound financial footing had made the transition from the medical and scientific to becoming places of entertainment while still keeping the appearance of respectability provided by museums. It was Barnum who fully embraced the idea of the museum as an amusement centre, and had the showmanship to exploit it. He took over the Scudder's American Museum on Broadway in New York City in 1841. Scudder's, a collection of poor, irrelevant art, stuffed animals, and skeletons, was failing. Barnum cleared these out, and made freaks the central attraction, although it was truly a house of varieties: industrious fleas, educated dogs, jugglers, ventriloquists, tableaux, gypsies, albinos, fat boys, giants, dwarfs, rope dancers, music, singing, dancing, models of the world's greatest cities, glass-blowing, knitting machines, warlike races, and religious ceremonies. It was presented as an amusing, funny, collection, and the disabled people, the freaks, were part of the fun and the amusement. Within a year Barnum had tripled the Museum's profits from their promotion, particularly of the freaks.

Despite this he managed to retain the respectability of the museum label, whilst getting pictures of his strangest exhibits into the pages of the *New York Herald* and *New York Tribune*. Indeed, his museum was so accepted that families would bring picnic lunches to spend the day there. It was an institution, said Barnum, where all the family 'could be educated and amused'. At the same time, Barnum added to his fortune by taking some of the exhibits on tour, most notably Tom Thumb. In 1844 the little man undertook a two year tour of Europe, ending with appearances at the Egyptian Hall in Piccadilly in the spring of 1846. In one week, General Tom Thumb attracted 12,000 people who paid a total of £600, a fortune in those days, to see him. The works of the well-known English artist Robert Haydon, who was displaying his work in another section of the Egyptian Halls, received attention from 133 people over the same period and produced the magnificent sum of £5.13s 6d. Haydon was so disgusted by the experience that he wrote in *The Times* of the 'Exquisite Feeling of the English People for High Art'. Deeply in debt he committed suicide a few weeks later, causing *The Times* to condemn Barnum and Tom Thumb: 'The display of a disgusting dwarf attracted hordes of gaping idiots, who poured into the pockets of a Yankee showman a stream of wealth one tithe of which would have redeemed an honourable English artist from wretchedness and death.'

It was showmen, like Barnum, who took a person or persons with a disability and transformed them into an 'attraction', mainly by giving them an appropriately exciting label. It was, indeed, the very names that set the scene, and created the curiosity. Often these were accompanied by outrageous accompanying stories about how the subjects acquired their distortions. Ella Harper – a young girl with severe orthopedic problems – became 'The Camel Girl'. In a newspaper interview Ella said: 'I am called The Camel Girl because my knees turn backwards. I can walk best on my hands and feet.'

The same 1886 interview indicated strongly that, in public at least, the freaks were not averse to profiting from their own disabilities, often regarding themselves as a branch of genuine show business: 'I have travelled considerably in show business for the past four years and now I intend to quit and go back to school and fit myself for another occupation,' said Ella Harper.

However, disabled people whose bodies had become contorted enough to be included, and for whom a suitably exciting billing – like the Camel Girl – could be dreamt-up, were generally unmercifully exploited. Museum advertisements and publicity handouts from the first half of the 19th century indicate there was no depth to which showmen would not sink to earn a dishonest crust: 'Casper Hauser, half man, half monkey'; 'Master Barber, the whiskered child'; 'Two snow white negroes'; 'Mlle Fanny, the connecting link between man and brute creation (actually an ape)'; Calvin Phillips, famous dwarf child'; The Elephant Man; the Sicilian Fairy; the Skeleton Dude; the Last of the Ancient Aztecs; the Transparent Man(whose body was so thin a light could be shone through it). If they could dream up a name for it, they displayed it. After a while freak shows acquired a predictable mix: the fat lady, the bearded lady, a giant, a dwarf, the skinniest man, albino families, india rubber men, human magnets, fireproof women, people who walked on fire, dozens of 'missing links' (the most famous of whom was Barnum's Zip, who was displayed for over 60 years).

These were combined with freaks from the darkest continents – 'cannibals', 'savages', pygmies, people with tribal distinctions like distended lips and extended necks. These shows displaying freaks from overseas led to further shameful deception and exploitation of physically disabled people and those with mental impairments. One exhibit – 'wild Australian children captured by Captain J. Reid' consisted, in fact, of mentally impaired children borrowed from an institution. They were Tom and Hettie, severely retarded siblings. Sadly they were put on show for over 30 years. Other exhibits featuring mentally retarded people included 'The Wild Man of Borneo', 'The Aztec Children' and even one titled just 'What is it?'.

Often the most sought after attractions were disabled people who could achieve remarkable feats despite their disabilities. There was The Human Trunk, a Russian named Nikolai Kobelkoff who was born without arms or legs. He started to appear in shows in the 1870s. His chief claim to fame was that he married a lady named Anna Wilfert and fathered eleven children. There were many 'armless wonders' who made up for what they lacked in upper limbs by using legs, feet and toes instead of arms. One of Barnum's early exhibits, Sanders Nellis, wound a watch, fired a pistol and fired a bow and arrow using his feet. Perhaps the most famous was Charles Tripp who appeared for more than half a century painting portraits, writing and doing carpentry before very large audiences. Ann Leak was so religious, despite her disability, that she embroidered and crocheted religious symbols. One of her stage lines was: 'So you perceive it's really true, when hands are lacking, toes will do.' Siamese twins became the most sought after attraction.

Typical were Violet and Daisy Hilton, joined at the buttocks, who were born in Brighton in 1908. They were sold to a showlady named Mary Hilton by their barmaid mother when they were two weeks old to be trained as freaks. The two girls were exported to America, where more money was available, and they appeared in Vaudeville productions in an act which featured them playing their own instruments and even dancing. At the height of their fame their publicity said they were earning around five thousand dollars a week for their 'owner'. It was not until 1931 that they successfully sued their guardian for their freedom and their rightful share of what she had earned from their talents.

Undoubtedly Barnum was the doyen of the showmen. It was he who came up with his famous attraction Tom Thumb, which, in turn, led to hundreds of imitations, like Major Mite, Harold Pyott, the English Tom Thumb, and Anita the Living Doll. However, perhaps Barnum's greatest accomplishment was his 'Lilliputian Congress of Nations', in which dozens of midgets took part.

Barnum also put some action into his shows, originating such ideas as midget weddings, births and other comic tricks, again soon to be imitated by others around the world. The famous Tom Thumb himself had many characters – Napoleon, Frederick the Great, Romulus, a Highlander, Villikin, a Courtier, a Sailor, a Citizen and Cain. When he appeared before Wellington, Tom Thumb was of course portrayed as Napoleon; when Wellington asked him why his Napoleon was so sad and thoughtful, Tom Thumb replied that it was because 'I was thinking of the loss of the Battle of Waterloo'.

By 1868, when a fire destroyed the American Museum, 41 million people had paid 25 cents each to walk through its doors.

After that Barnum gave up museums, and diversified into travelling shows. However, there were imitators aplenty of his former specialty, with the dime museums, charging ten cents as their title implies, leading the way. Taking up Barnum's baton, they proliferated from 1870, and reached their peak in the last decade of the century. Most American cities boasted at least one, and New York, particularly in the Bowery area, had fifty or more. Boston, Philadelphia and Chicago were almost as well served, and there were even national chains of dime shows, facilitating ease and economies in the booking of exhibitors. The freak or human oddity continued to be the main attraction at the dime museums, and their origins and stories were even more distorted and exaggerated to meet the growing competition, not only from other dime shows but also circus side shows and other amusement places. The genuine 'freak sensations' acquired great fame, attracted large crowds, and earned a lot of money. 'The Dog Faced Boy', a man whose body was covered by hair was such a draw in New York City that he was put on show twenty-three times a day. The demand for new attractions was such that managers sent out freak hunters to search the world for new sensations.

Live shows were not the only form of such 'entertainment'. Many exhibitions, mainly contained in small shops, displayed curiosities in jars. In Watts Phillips' 'The Wild Tribes of London' written in 1855, he describes such an exhibition in Ship Alley in the East End of London:

> 'But, speaking of the shops, we must not omit some mention of one certainly peculiar in its appearance…It is a dingy, sinister-looking shop bearing the ambitious name of the British and Foreign Medicine Institution, and its proprietor rejoices in the rather ominous title of Dr Graves. Our business, however, is with the window and its collection of horrors…wax models of terrible diseases…bottled babies aplenty, children with two heads, a serpent taken from the body of a sailor, and a skeleton of a small sailor, taken from the body of a serpent, with other horrors too numerous to mention.'

By 1908 Barnum said he was eliminating his freak department. The main reason given was 'that large number of letters received criticising exhibitions of human abnormalities… and expressing the wish that something more elevating might be substituted'. To a large extent this was an attempt to gain publicity for the shows, for he continued them for many years afterwards.

However, freak shows were in slow decline. Their final demise was not seen until the nineteen forties in the United States. It came about not only because public tastes changed but because the medical profession began to classify what was wrong with the freaks and with knowledge came the death of curiosity and the feeling that it might not be the done thing to gawp and, even worse, laugh.

In March 1908 an article in the *Scientific American* acknowledged this trend:

'The announcement from Ansonia, Conn. of the recent death of the only living skeleton, directs attention to the entire class of freaks, or human prodigies, as they themselves prefer to be called. They have for the medical man a more than ordinary and passing interest. Most of these humble and unfortunate individuals whose sole means of livelihood is the exhibition of their physical infirmities to a gaping and unsympathetic crowd, are rarities worthy of more serious study than they usually receive.

'Their mortality rate is high, and many of those recently most famous are already dead or have been retired from public view by chronic invalidism. A few days ago there retired in Chicago Maggie Minott, one of the most extraordinary of the anaosomes, or true dwarfs. She was twenty-seven inches high and weighed twenty-five pounds. Most of these pigmies are types of infantilism. An exception was the comparatively robust and virile Tom Thumb, who had a vigorous and manly beard.

'Bass, the ossified man, also died several years ago. He was a man of unusual intelligence, and his condition was caused by an extreme degree of *polyarthritis deformans*. He was injured by a careless museum attendant who let him fall as he was being removed from a carriage, and he never fully recovered. The elastic skin man a few years ago contracted tuberculous disease of the lungs from exposure of his scantily clad body on the drafty stage of dime museums. His was a case of generalised dermatolysis, and had an amusing trick of drawing the skin of his forehead down over his face like a veil.

Closely allied to him was the Russian dog-faced man, with features marvellously resembling those of a Scotch terrier. He and the bearded lady, who was wont to convince the most sceptical by a liberal but chaste display of the matronly charms of her rounded and well-developed figure, were unusual examples of hypertrichosis. The blonde loveliness of the Circassian beauty, who delighted our unsophisticated younger days, was, of course, a case of albinoism, and the wild men of Borneo and Barnum's is what we now recognise, in the maturer years of professional experience, as cases of microcephalous idiocy, gathered for the most part from the negro population of our southern plantations.

'Most examples of gigantism are cases of acromegaly, as was notably Chang, the Chinese giant, he of the gentle, emotional temperament and, in his last days, the excessive muscular debility so characteristic of this disease. The various human pin cushions who have been on exhibition could doubtless present for the neurologist curious areas of anaesthesia and analgesia, which he would probably refer to as finite lesions in the spinal cord.

'Many students of the late Dr E.C.Sequin's will remember the blue man whom he often showed in his grey hue, approaching the colour of a maltese cat, due to the argyria of his tissues produced by the prolonged administration of silver nitrate, a melancholy victim of credulity as to the efficacy of this drug in locomotor ataxia.

'In parts of southern Europe there was formerly plied a nefarious trade in maiming and mutilating young children for the purpose of producing distressing deformities to excite pity and thus induce alms. An instance of such mutilation is made romantic use of by Victor Hugo in his story *L'Homme qui rit*. In most civilised countries there are now enacted laws forbidding the public exhibition of monsters and revolting deformities. A more refined and humane public taste now frowns upon such exhibitions, and they are less profitable for their promoters.

'The profession of museum freak is passing. The genuine Iusus naturae is, however, always a valuable subject of study for the scientific physician, which may add to our knowledge of development of normal types and may possibly illuminate many difficult and obscure problems in pathology.'

Victorian times saw the greatest growth in the exhibition of disabled people for amusement and profit. This continued well into the twentieth century, particularly in the United States. As late as 1932 Hollywood produced a film with the title 'Freaks – the story of the love life of the sideshow'. Freak shows only began to disappear when medical science explained human differences and what caused disabilities. Of course, we are not blameless today. In 'horror' films the association of evil with disability is still common. Films like 'The Elephant Man', whilst purporting to show the Victorian fascination with the weird and wonderful in human beings, also provided much to amuse today's audiences.

Chapter Six

Children

Disabled children have always led a precarious existence, but never so much as in the Greco-Roman period whether at birth, as the victims of the 'exposure' policy (referred to earlier), or as convenient offerings for sacrifice. However, as Roman attitudes gave way to the advance in Christianity, edicts of Constantine I forbade infanticide, maiming children as beggars or selling them into slavery. At the same time he put in place measures to help parents too poor to support their children, and laws which enabled formal adoption. In AD 325 the Council of Nicaea made it compulsory for each village to have a hostelry for poor and disabled people. Many such hostels became asylums for children. Although infanticide of disabled children was still widespread, parents were told to leave deformed or unwanted babies at a church, rather than 'expose' them precipitating death. Later, the Council of Vaison, AD 442, decreed a time of sanctuary for abandoned children while efforts were made to find their parents.

Despite this slightly more humane approach, the overwhelming feeling of most parents of disabled children was one of shame, and their instinct was to hide them. It was an attitude that persisted well into the twentieth century, and into the higher echelons of society. The British television documentary 'The Lost Prince' described how the brother of Edward VIII and George VI, born with epilepsy, was hidden and locked away. When the boy died Edward VIII remarked on what a blessing it was.

After the Roman empire fell into decay and finally ended, other provision for children began to emerge. The first foundling home was established in 786 by the Archbishop of Milan, Daltheus, and such institutions proliferated throughout Europe, although the children taken into them did not fare well; most of them died of contagious diseases or neglect. Spiritually children were not let off lightly: St.Augustine said that children had inherent propensities for evil and had to be redeemed from their sinful state which existed from birth. This doctrine of original sin had profound implications for children with disabilities. They were no longer holy innocents, but represented punishment for the sins of their fathers or were creatures of Satan. This later inference brought the *Malleus Maleficarum*, The Witches Hammer, a textbook published in 1487, written by Johann Sprenger and Heinrich Kraemer, two monks appointed by Pope Innocent VIII as inquisitors of heretical depravities. That publication became the code on witchcraft for at least two centuries, with severe consequences for disabled children. Those with seizures, unusual behaviour of any kind, particularly those that we would now describe as having learning difficulties, were judged to be in league with Satan. For many it resulted in trial and execution. This attitude persisted even into the Reformation and filtered into new religious beliefs: both Luther and Calvin judged that retarded children were controlled by Satan.

The abandonment of disabled children continued, but in more subtle forms. In the seventh century and beyond, came the practice of 'oblatio', meaning offering. Under this children could be offered to the Church as oblates by their parents. The children from better-off families were later able to take vows and become monks or priests whilst those from the not so well off became labourers in church communities. Whether children could be forced to remain oblates became a matter of controversy in the ninth century, but nevertheless many of them were. The records of one English monastery in a forty year period in the eleventh century show that over eighty per cent of its monks had been oblates.

There are other strong indications that children with disabilities were more likely than others to be offered for monastic life. Jerome complained that 'parents dedicated to virginity those daughters who are deformed or defective in some way'. Ulrich of Cluny in the eleventh century wrote of 'parents who commit to monasteries any hump-backed, deformed, dull or unpromising children they have'. The church readily took what can only be described as bribes to accept disabled children. It was obligatory to offer money or land before they would take in 'the lame, the malformed, the one-eyed, the squinting, the blind, the crippled.'

Later, as oblatio declined in the churches, a similar pattern developed with abandoned children being offered to the growing number of wealthier families for training as household workers and servants. The giving of children to others to train and educate continued, but now they went to noblemen's courts. The custom was so widespread that the period from the 4th to the 13th century has been given the label of the 'abandonment mode'. There were other methods of achieving abandonment. Wet nursing was a particular favourite. Only about a quarter of the wet nurses lived in with the bourgeois families they served, which meant that the other three-quarters of the children were farmed out to the homes of the wet nurses themselves. Many of the children, particularly if they proved as they grew to be disabled, were never reclaimed.

By the 14th century a more specialised approach to the abandonment of disabled children developed through a network of foundling homes. One of the first was the San Gallo in Florence, followed by others in Italy, France and Germany. The number of children left at these hospices grew rapidly between the 14th and 16th centuries. By the 18th century over five thousand children a year, many of them disabled, were being abandoned at the Paris hospice founded by Vincent de Paul. Abandonments reached up to 43% of all births in Florence, 25% in Milan, and 25% in France.

Some disabilities were caused by crude methods and lack of care at childbirth. In the sixteenth and seventeenth centuries maternity was often a dangerous nightmare. In England, infant mortality was in the region of 130 per 1000 live births (as compared with a figure today of around 9 per 1000), but no figures are available of the number of children and mothers caused permanent disability. Most often, untrained women were in charge, with the barber-surgeon only being called in to remove a dead foetus from the womb. Occasionally, too, these same 'surgeons', those who on the whole served only the well-to-do, would open a woman dying during labour to save an unborn child, but there is no record of any woman surviving these first Caesarean operations.

The midwives were customarily impatient, to the extent of being uncaring. They had a tendency in cases of long labour of pulling hard on a limb of the unborn child, sometimes tugging it off altogether. In Paris, by the seventeenth century, there were the first glimmers of hope for the unfortunate expectant mothers. Louise Bourgeois acquired fame by bringing Marie de Medici, wife of Henry IV, through six successful confinements and published a textbook, 'The Compleat Midwife's Practice Enlarged', in 1659. She also began the first formal training of midwives. By 1679 midwives in Amsterdam had to attend obstetrics classes. In England in 1687 Elizabeth Cellier asked James II for permission to set-up a lying-in hospital to be run by trained midwives, but the College of Physicians objected and it never happened.

Men began to take more of an interest in maternity. Books by them appeared describing ectopic pregnancy and Caesarean section, and one of the volumes, 'Treatise on the Illnesses of Pregnant Women' by Frenchman Francois Mauriceau at last attacked the myth prevalent among both physicians and midwives that the pelvic bones separated during labour to make the birth easier.

In Britain, the traditional woman midwife was also gradually replaced by a male version known as a man-midwife. They were qualified medical practitioners who possessed and used instruments, particularly the new forceps. Doyen among them was William Smellie who lived from 1697 until 1763. He was trained in Paris, but came to London in 1739. Smellie redesigned the forceps, and wrote a guide called simply '*Midwifery*'. However, Smellie's pupil, William Hunter, was the one who spread the word: he gave lectures and trained the surgeon-obstetricians who began to spread into British provincial towns. Some enlightenment followed. New born babies were no longer swaddled, because the new male practitioners believed it was healthier for them to be able to move and exercise their limbs. Wet nurses became unfashionable, as the men persuaded well-to-do ladies that it was healthier and better for them to breast feed their own children.

Unfortunately, such enlightenment did not extend to unwanted children, particularly those deformed or disabled. In England between 1700 and 1825, 154 foundling hospitals were created to reduce the high rate of infant mortality and to provide care for 'bastard and poor children'. Schools for rejected children, as portrayed by Dickens' Dotheboys Hall, often charitable, were not uncommon in the mid-19th century, and they also provided a means of abandoning disabled and unwanted children. The first English schools for children with physical disabilities were established in 1851 in Marylebone, London, and in Kensington in 1865. In the 1860s a 'cripples nursery' was started in London, in which the children were trained in such trades as jewellery and boot making.

The risks for children in these foundling hospices were high, largely through exposure to communicable disease. Common illnesses included influenza, bronchial diseases, measles, smallpox, dehydration, tuberculosis, diphtheria, bowel and urinary tract problems, tumours, hernias, carbuncles and sores which did not heal. Estimates of the number of children who died in their first year of life in French and London foundling homes in the 17th and 18th centuries ranged from 33 to 90 per cent. The first influence of science began to appear, but was of little immediate help. Childhood diseases like chickenpox, smallpox, whooping cough and scarlet fever and the disabilities they caused were identified and written up in textbooks, but this knowledge had no effect on the treatment most children received, purging still being the most common form of recommended remedy.

Growing alongside the foundling hospices were those other symbols of abandonment, the workhouses, into which many children went with their very poor families. These had come about largely because of the shift from rural to urban communities during the Industrial Revolution and the rapid growth of towns. At times of famine in particular, armies of the poor came into the towns seeking food. Many begged in the streets. A few relief measures were taken, but mainly the attitude of the authorities was to get the homeless and poor off the streets and out of sight and hearing.

In England the Poor Laws resulted in the founding of almshouses for the poor, the disabled and the undesirable. The English Poor Laws between 1563 and 1601 decreed that they would be funded by local taxes. In what came to be known as 'the workhouse', the occupants were condemned to forced labour. There was thus a high concentration of the mad, the poor and the delinquent in one place. Germany had similar establishments, the Zuchthäuser, and in France there were Maisons de Force.

Public attitudes and fears about the workhouse as a place for the poor and disabled people are summed up in Will Carleton's 1897 poem *Over The Hill to the Poor House*:

'What is the use of heapin' on me a pauper's shame?
Am I lazy or crazy? am I blind or lame?
True, I am not so supple, nor yet so awful stout;
But charity ain't no favour, if one can live without.'

There was still extreme ignorance about the causes of childhood disability. A sixteenth century French surgeon, Ambroise Pare, produced a textbook on childhood disabilities called *'Montres et Prodiges'*. He said there were thirteen causes of birth defects, many of them reflecting the superstitions which still existed, seemingly even among the medical profession. He wrote that couples should not engage in sexual relationships during menstruation, lactation, Lent or on Sundays. If they did the result could be lameness, leprosy, deformity, seizures, or the death of any child produced as a result of any congress at those times.

The fear and suspicion of disabled children, and perhaps more importantly, the sense of shame they brought upon their families which caused them to be abandoned into institutions, persisted for centuries. There were also many instances of hiding children from the outside world, locking them in rooms, cupboards, and even cages.

Perhaps the most shocking example happened in the United States. Josiah Jnr, the eldest son of the Rev. Josiah Spaulding, was born in Buckland, Massachusetts in 1786. Although he studied and seemed bright, he displayed behaviour which marked him as a 'raving maniac', according to his father. Ashamed, they first kept him shackled but when he escaped from this impediment they locked him in a cage and he remained there for over five decades. He was kept naked, except that he was provided with a blanket to wrap round himself. From the day Josiah was put into the cage, it is recorded that his 'grieving' father never again mentioned the boy to his friends or his congregation.

When his father and mother both died in 1823, his sister Lydia, who had married a Mr.Howes, reluctantly agreed to have her now thirty-year-old brother under her roof. The naked and chained Josiah was led from the parsonage into his new residence followed by four men carrying his dismantled cage. This was re-assembled in the back upstairs bedroom of the house. In 1828 Mr.Howes discovered that the town was required by law to care for maniacs, and he approached them on Josiah's behalf. The selectmen of the town were reluctant to place him in the almshouse or in the county jail, which would have been normal in such cases, so they came to an agreement with Mr.Howes that he continued to 'care' for him, for which they would pay fifty-two dollars and exempt him from taxation during Josiah's natural lifetime.

Then Lydia died, leaving Josiah to the mercy of Mr.Howes. He, true to his agreement with the town, continued to care for the caged man, who was now fifty years old. The next year Howes married again, and it was his new wife Lois who showed Josiah the only real affection he would have received in his lifetime, cooking his favourite foods and spending time with him. There was a notable change in his behaviour. Howes died in 1855, but Lois continued to look after Josiah, who was now sixty-nine-years old and had by then been in a cage for forty-five years.

When Lois died in 1864, he was transferred to the town poor farm, (workhouse). His cage went with him and he was put straight back into it. He became a curiosity. People came from miles around to see the 'disgusting and revolting maniac'. The demand became such that the proprietors of the workhouse conducted tours, and the visitors were told that the caged man was treated like an animal because he acted like one.

Josiah died on Christmas Eve 1867. He was laid in an unmarked grave, but he was given an epitaph in the town records: 'Josiah Spaulding, Jnr, died December 24th 1867. Unmarried, he was for many years insane; and tenderly cared for by his family.'

Medical attitudes towards children and their disabilities were improving with the development of paediatrics as a specialty. French physician Nicholas Andry (1658-1742) warned that the improper care of babies could be responsible for later deformities. In England the first major contribution came from Michael Underwood in 1784 with his *'Treatise on the Diseases of Children'*. Outpatient dispensaries for children began to spring up where free treatment was offered to the poor.

Congenital conditions, particularly club foot, began to receive attention. Jacques Delpech in France tried to put club foot right by sectioning the Achilles tendon. In Germany, Georg Stromeyer carried out a tenotomy on a club foot with success. He advanced the idea of sectioning the tendon for all deformities caused by muscular defects, and so became the father of modern or-thopaedic surgery. The method spread to England through one William John Little, himself club footed, who went to study Stromeyer's methods. So convinced did he become that he underwent a successful subcutaneous tenotomy, and, cured of his disability, returned to London to perform the operation himself. In 1854, the invention of the quick-drying Plaster of Paris by Anthonius Mathijsen enabled the correction of many deformities by encouraging limbs to develop straight in growing children. However, in some conditions, where the need for exercise and movement was not understood, the invention led to more children becoming disabled than were saved from it.

Segregation and isolation was the lot of disabled children in the nineteenth century; more and more institutions, mainly charitable, were set-up in which many of the children were trained in some basic trade – usually boot mending for boys and needlecraft for girls. They were given little or no contact with other children, or even adults. The exclusion of disabled children from ordinary life continued in more subtle ways well into the twentieth century. Ironically, one of the objects of Alf Morris' famous 'Chronically Sick and Disabled Persons Act 1970' resulting in the "construction of over thirty specialist hospital units for disabled children and young people", was to get them out of geriatric wards, at that time the current dustbin for disabled children because there was nowhere else to put them (Chapter XII).

The isolation of disabled children in the twentieth century was seen also in the development of specialist schools for almost every childhood disability, deafness, blindness, autism, the lame, the mentally handicapped, and in some specialties these survive. It was not really until the 1980s that integration became the buzzword, and with it pressure to establish units within mainstream schools, in which specialist needs could be met but where there would still be contact with other children, with genuine awakening of awareness on each side. The Education Act 1981 decreed that children with learning difficulties, no less than other disabled children, must be educated in mainstream schools or classes wherever possible.

Chapter Seven

Mental Health – Socio-Medical Development

The obsessive association of "madmen" with evil and that supreme symbol of evil, the devil, took its first grip early in man's history and persists across the centuries. In most early civilisations people were afraid of the extreme behaviour caused by mental illness and acted accordingly to protect themselves and their possessions. Down the ages of British treatment of mentally incapacitated people, the labels used to describe it may have varied but until very recently the fear remained. Earlier generations knew them simply as fools, idiots, village idiots, innocents, mad, lunatic, distracted, crazy, stupid. Even by the time the Mental Deficiency Act 1913 had reached the Statute Book, the labels had become no kinder. This referred to morons, idiotism, imbeciles, the feeble-minded and the moral imbecile or moral defective. From then through to the 1950's, the terms mental defective and mental deficiency were largely accepted, followed by the use, starting in the United States, of the term sub-normal. In the late 'fifties terms like mental disorder and backward came into vogue. In the 'seventies mentally handicapped became the fashion, followed closely by people with mental handicap. In 1986 the term 'people with learning difficulties' was widely adopted.

Of all types of disability, the harshest treatment has been reserved for people disabled in mind. In Graeco-Roman law, insanity was a family responsibility. As a result, most sufferers were imprisoned in their own homes so that they did no damage to others or to property. In some cases, so as to prevent blame and punishment falling on their families, they were set free to wander. These poor souls were far from popular since Romans believed that the spirits with which they were possessed could come out of them and possess other people. Hippocratic medicine explained madness in terms of humours like bile: melancholy madness was said to be caused by black bile. Galen asserted that mania was caused by yellow bile. Some physicians came closer to some of today's understanding: Soranus blamed continual sleeplessness, excesses of venery, anger, grief, anxiety, superstitious fear, shock or a blow, or intense straining of the senses. All acknowledged that there was very little that could be done for those afflicted mentally.

Even the humane Felix Platter (1536-1614), one of the first specialists in the field of mental problems, concluded that madness was the 'handiwork of the devil'. All early work in the area suffered from the fact that those trying to help usually failed to separate the insane from the mentally deficient.

In England very early on it was accepted that all that could be done for most of those afflicted was to shut them away to protect themselves and others. The first institution for achieving this was the infamous Bethlem, founded as the Priory of the Order of St. Mary of Bethlehem in London in 1247. It was first described as a hospital in 1329, but was seized by the state in 1375 as a place to put lunatics. Shortly afterwards, in 1403, there was an official enquiry into corruption after the warden embezzled money from the relatives and friends of the patients, which set the scene for the rest of the asylum's chequered history. Growing demand for its services led to its being rebuilt in 1676 on a new site which could accommodate up to 150 inmates. Designed based on the Tuileries in Paris, it acquired the nickname of Bedlam, a word which has established itself in the English language. It proved to be of great amusement to the general populace: patients representing raving or melancholy madness were cheered by crowds who gathered around the entrance gates. Samuel Johnson records going to Bedlam with a party for amusement. It says something about the way mentally disabled people were treated that Bethlem remained the only specialised establishment for the insane until the 17th century.

As with the ancients, people judged to be mad were a family responsibility. If a family did not exist or was unable to cope, a community might provide a custodian or put them into safekeeping in a jail. In England in the seventeenth and eighteenth centuries, the mentally ill and disabled were expected to be cared for at home with very occasional and hard–won parish relief being available to support the families involved.

The Elizabethan Poor Law had laid down that it was relatives who should pay for the relief of the disabled and the poor. If families had things that might be sold to help care for a disabled member, the parish was entitled to take the necessary action. When a mentally disabled parishioner's parents died, the parish sold off anything they left behind to defray the costs of providing whatever they could for the surviving offspring. There were also many who roamed the countryside as vagabonds, where, again, it was often parishes who provided relief, or referred them on to madhouses. Parish records show relief to people labelled as 'fools', 'naturals', 'distracted', 'mad', 'lunatick', 'ideott', and so on. Parishes sometimes financed the nursing and lodging of mentally disabled people, either by means of providing parish nurses or by paying for the lodgings with professional landlords and landladies or with a member of the parish. A class of carers described as nurses, developed who were called upon regularly to care for sick and poor people.

In some European countries monasteries became the place where madmen could be placed: out of mind and out of sight. In the late eighteenth century in England the concept of the madhouse developed to provide a similar service. Most of them were privately run and had no medical basis. Some were religious or community charities. The policy was to find convenient dustbins and the opportunities for families and communities to rid themselves of disliked or eccentric individuals. Medical men did not play a great part in judging people to be mad and suitable candidates for the madhouse: it was left to communities and families who could no longer cope and were able to pay for the privilege of having the responsibility of care taken from their hands. The most violent inmates were strait-jacketed, manacled and chained to walls.

There were many theories about insanity. The philosopher Descartes ruled that madness could not be placed in the soul or the mind so had to have its roots in the body. His teaching encouraged a search for the site of madness within the brain itself.

In England, after intense observation of the nervous system, Thomas Willis produced his *'Anatomy of the Brain'* in 1664, followed in 1667 by *'Pathology of the Brain'*, and *'Specimen of the Nature of the Nerves'*, which made suggestions about the origins of insanity, epilepsy, asthma, and apoplexy. Despite his attempts at a scientific approach, he still believed that animal spirits were intermediaries between body and mind. He also believed that maniacs should be restrained.

In society at large, the mad were not identified as a separate group, as distinct from the great number of rootless poor, under the vagrancy laws, until the 1714 Act. Consequently many of them roamed the countryside, staying at workhouses, suffering punishment for not working. The age of real growth of the madhouse was the eighteenth century. A charitable asylum was established in Norwich in 1713, and a ward for incurable lunatics at Guys Hospital in 1728. St.Lukes' charitable asylum was founded in London in 1751, another in Newcastle-upon-Tyne in 1764, followed quickly by still others in Manchester, Northampton, York, Leicester, and Hereford. A separate trade in 'private' lunacy developed through which people who could afford to pay had relatives hidden away. In England the Madhouse Act 1774 did set up rudimentary licensing and certification with magistrates empowered to carry out writs to put people into custody. Previously, the madhouse had been a secret place, largely concealed from scrutiny. The Act met with opposition from vested medical interests who feared the profitability of private asylums would be threatened.

Reforms sought by Daniel Defoe advocated that the mentally defective and the insane should be separated, but also warned that unscrupulous people were putting away relatives, particularly wives, in institutions. Defoe's idea for licensed institutions did not reach the statute book until the 1774 Act. But it did little to improve the welfare of the inmates of madhouses. The insane continued to be badly treated, with the additional humiliation that they came to be looked upon as comic. People went to watch lunatics as they might go to a monkey house in a zoo, or freaks in a show.

The great majority, those lacking means, were herded together in brutal conditions, with no heat, no clothes, and with frostbite commonly reported. Inmates were chained to walls and gagged if they became violent or awkward. Nothing that could reasonably be described as treatment was given, though many physicians advocated, and gave, duckings in cold water or 'bled' to the point of physical exhaustion.

The first changes to this crude approach to madness did not come until the nineteenth century, when doctors at last began to see it as another facet of medicine and tried to find methods of treating patients as well as keeping them 'safe'. Brislington House, built in 1806 in Bristol, became Britain's first purpose-built asylum. Although it was a place for the well-to-do patients, it provided for segregation of inmates according to the severity of their illness, and did away with most of the methods of restraint. The lead in this latter respect had been given by the French physician Philippe Pinel (1745-1826), who decided that the first stage of treatment should be to release patients from their chains. For him this reform was a gradual process, with the chains not being removed all at once but over a period of time. He was successful, and eventually all patients in his care lost their shackles.

His '*Medico-philosophical Treatise on Mental Alienation*', based on hard clinical observation, was translated into many languages, including English, and greatly influenced physicians trying for the first time to treat madness. He stressed mental over physical causes. His 'moral treatment' was also directed at the emotions. He retained the traditional division of madness into melancholia, mania, idiocy, and dementia, but he developed new categories including partial and affective insanity. He judged them all to be incurable but held that melancholy and mania could respond to moral methods. He suggested that madmen could be distracted from their deluded imagination by diverting their minds, through shock, engaging them in labour, or by getting them to act out their delusions. Pinel argued the case for a reformed asylum system in which the inmates could be studied and helped.

In England William Cullen (1710-90) defined insanity as a dynamic neurological disorder, but thought madness was a false association of ideas. George III, if one were needed, provided a lesson that madness was no respecter of persons.

After the king's first attack in 1788, a Revd. Dr Francis Willis, who ran an asylum in Lincolnshire, was called in. He believed that madness was the result of over excitement and advocated that the unfortunate George be allowed a long period of calmness and control. He achieved this by putting him into a straitjacket and a restraining chair and pushing a gag into his mouth. Six months later the king seemed to have recovered and Willis was granted a pension of £1000 a year for 21 years by the Prime Minister, William Pitt. Since George, we know now, was suffering from porphyria, a hereditary disease of the metabolism which results in mental confusion and stomach pains, the recovery could only have been a temporary one, and nothing at all to do with the good 'madhouse doctor' from Lincolnshire.

Unsurprisingly now, all treatments then were of scant help and most sufferers were banished to the madhouse. There was no national basis or code of conduct for the treatment of those who found themselves in these institutions. Many were run as charities and what happened in them was at the mercy of their trustees most of whom, having very little knowledge about mental health, reflected public fear of the insane. The treatment received by many inmates, particularly the poor, was appallingly inhumane. The well-to-do, however, often received better treatment. The saviour of George III, the clergyman Francis Willis, ran an extraordinary establishment. Using the theory of control which seemed to work so well for the king, he created a madhouse in which all patients undertook controlled work – as labourers and agricultural workers – dressed immaculately in black coats, black silk breeches, stockings and a white waistcoat. Each of them also sported a powdered wig.

Most madhouses enjoyed no such refinements, and conditions began to cause disquiet even in those crude times. In 1814 a Yorkshire magistrate, Godfrey Higgins, drew attention to what was happening at the York Lunatic Asylum. On one of his visits as a Governor to the institution he found thirteen women in a cell twelve feet by just under eight feet. He reported that 144 deaths had been concealed, and he demanded an official enquiry which brought to light evidence of the widespread use of chains and other types of restraint, corruption of funds, filth and neglect, murder and rape.

An asylum called the York Retreat developed its own form of treatment called moral management which had as its basis the belief that madness could be corrected by a superior will. Opened by William Tuke and Quakers after the mysterious death in 1790 of Hannah Mills, a Quaker patient in York Lunatic Asylum, it afforded comfort and support. Patients and staff lived, ate and worked together in a model of family life. There was a solid carrot-and-stick approach, with rewards and punishment. No medicine was available or given. Samuel Tuke, William's grandson, described in 1813 the 'moral treatment' given to patients. 'Authority and order must be maintained', he wrote 'but these are better maintained by kindness, condescension, and indulgent attention, than by any severities whatsoever'. This approach appeared to meet with some success. In its first fifteen years, the York Retreat recorded curing – defined as people who were not readmitted to an asylum – 21 out of 31 cases of mania and 19 out of 30 cases of melancholia where the insanity was of recent origin. In longstanding cases they discharged 10 out of 61 patients suffering from mania and 6 out of 21 patients with melancholia. Tuke gave these facts and a description of the York Retreat's work to a Parliamentary Select Committee on Madhouses in 1815.

Evidence given to the committee made many people realise at last that there was a group of disabled and helpless people who were chained, beaten, sometimes starved. Some assessment could be made of the extent that the York Retreat was ahead of its time by evidence given to the same Committee of continuing maltreatment at the Bethlem Hospital. A group of Members of Parliament investigated the infamous regime there. Their evidence to the Select Committee drew a cruel and dismal picture in which patients were restrained by means of an iron ring rivetted round the neck, from which a short chain passed through another ring which slid upwards and downwards on an upright six-foot iron bar inserted into the wall. Round the body an iron frame was rivetted. On each side of the bar there was a circular projection, which enclosed each of the arms, keeping them close to the sides. It was perhaps some comfort that Thomas Monro, the physician at the hospital, in his evidence reassured the MPs present that such methods of restraint were for 'pauper lunatics', not for gentlemen lunatics, whose families presumably could afford something better! The Bethlem hospital itself was exposed as being 'badly mismanaged and appalling'. It employed only four people to look after over a hundred patients. The inspecting parliamentarians found that many inmates were left naked or covered only with a blanket. Ten women were found chained by one arm or one leg to the wall, naked except for a blanket gown which did not fasten. In the cells down below, the investigators came across a patient called James Norris who had been kept in Bethlem for over ten years – nobody knew exactly how long – in a specially made iron restraint which meant that he could only lie on his back and move a foot to either side.

The imprisonment, for that was what it was, of the insane in madhouses presented medicine with a challenge. Here were whole blocks, communities, of tortured humanity about whom little was understood, and for whom no satisfactory treatment existed. Some medical men decided that they needed to demonstrate that madness was a medical condition which, one day, would be treatable. A growing number of 'mad doctors' appeared intent on proving that insanity was rooted in the brain.

In England the insane represented such a national problem that an Act of Parliament in 1808 allowed local authorities to use the rates, even to increase them, to build lunatic asylums 'for the mad poor'. The result was so patchy and many of the asylums were of such poor quality that there were a great many scandals concerning the treatment of the inmates, with the result that the Metropolitan Commissioners in Lunacy were set-up in 1828 to police asylums.

The 'mad doctors' were struggling to gain public respect. In 1841 they managed to establish their own professional body – the Association of Medical Officers of Asylums and Hospitals for the Insane. This changed its name with changing nomenclature for madness and eventually, in 1971, became the Royal College of Psychiatrists.

Whether it was because there were now more 'mad doctors' to diagnose insanity or whether there was indeed an increase, the problem appeared to be growing. By 1844 there were 21,000 patients, 80% of them paupers, held in asylums and 139 private madhouses. It was Lord Ashley, later to become Lord Shaftesbury, whose campaigning led to the 1845 the Lunatic Act which made it mandatory for each county to build an asylum for the 'pauper insane'. It also gave the Metropolitan Commissioners in Lunacy the power to inspect all institutions in which the insane were kept. Ashley, as Chairman of the Lunacy Commission, was able to oversee the implementation of the Act. A new concept of mental nursing emerged which at last laid emphasis on the treatment of the person no longer as mad and dangerous but as a sick individual who could be helped. The old methods of treatment, largely by bleeding and purging, began to disappear. Restraint, using manacles and straight jackets, also decreased considerably. Some of the English 'mad doctors' – notably Robert Gardner Hill at the Lincoln Asylum and John Conolly at the Hanwell Asylum – at last began to follow the example set earlier by Pinel and stopped using restraint. In 1856 Conolly wrote a textbook called *'Treatment of the Insane without Mechanical Restraints'* which greatly influenced other early psychiatrists.

The description 'lunatic' was replaced by 'insane' but no distinction was made between the mentally ill and the mentally defective. At Hanwell, the largest asylum in England, they even began educational classes. Although the numbers of people in asylums were rising, largely because there were now more asylum places, others were still just disappearing into the community: Andrew Doyle, an inspector of the Poor Law Board, in 1853 claimed that of the 126,000 inmates in workhouses, over 6,000 were known to be insane.

There were considerable doubts about the level of competence of those caring for patients. Nursing staff were largely untrained and received very low recompense for their long hours of toil. Only one establishment – St.Luke's Hospital, London – provided teaching for medical students on the treatment of mental disorders.

In 1870 the average number of people in an asylum was 542; by 1900, it had become 961; and by 1930 it was 1,221. It was like housing an army, with large but overcrowded wards, and standards of care inevitably were poor.

This largely meant that as new understanding and treatments developed, the asylums were by-passed, their natural home now being the consulting room – for the well-to-do – and a few out-patients departments. On this field of play, the view that insanity could be treated through moral therapy was challenged as more practitioners began to believe that some madness had a physical cause. Austrian doctors in particular offered the 'science' of phrenology as a means of defining the physical aspects. They held that the brain was the organ of thought and will, and that the exercise of its various parts led to these parts changing, shaping the brain and the personality. The reading of the bumps thus caused, determined this personality.

In the asylums there was very little actual treatment, other than providing a community atmosphere, although some asylum superintendents tried shock treatment – like cold baths and electric shocks. A large literature of learned books containing observations of the insane and what effect these 'treatments' had on them was published.

There were continuing scandals about how the asylums were run and the conditions in which patients were kept. So much so that other types of institutions appeared, like nerve clinics and rest homes for people who could afford to avoid the stigma of the asylums. They had such low esteem in the public mind that even then there were murmurings, some from medical men, questioning whether this was the best approach for dealing with the insane, and suggesting that the finance involved might be better spent paying for families to care for them in the community.

One thing the asylums did do was to provide a large community of mentally afflicted people in one place and this helped psychiatrists to produce classifications of mental diseases, which brought the real beginnings of diagnosis. For the first time, for instance, epileptics began to be separated from the insane. Knowledge was growing. The asylums also led some practitioners to the pessimistic approach which became known as degeneration. They were now full of people most of whom, having entered them, never left. Their problems were seen as irreversible. Some psychiatrists, particularly in France, began to look into the backgrounds of patients and found hereditary traits, leading to the theory that some forms of insanity developed gradually over generations, ending in imbecility. According to Saint-Yon Morel in his treatise '*Physical and Moral Degeneration*' published in 1857, family histories passed from nervous hysteria through to alcoholic or narcotic addiction, criminality, prostitution, then to insanity proper followed by idiocy. To help prove his case, Morel pointed out that alcoholism was widespread among pauper madmen.

Degenerative ideas caught on, particularly related to sexuality and homosexuality. In England they were taken up by Dr Henry Maudsley, among others, who made possible the Maudsley Hospital, later to become the Institute of Psychiatry, through a legacy. Impossible though it might appear against the dismal and depressing backcloth created by the asylums, the first brief nod in the direction of community and after care had begun. When Dr Maudsley offered £30,000 to the London County Council to make possible a new mental hospital, he did so primarily on the conditions that it was to treat early and acute cases, that it would have an outpatients clinic, and that it would also undertake teaching and research. It opened in 1915 and a special parliamentary sanction was obtained to make it possible for the hospital to accept patients without certification under the 1890 Act. Its work with civilians was delayed because during the war it was used largely to treat shell-shocked troops, recognised as a form of seriously disabling mental illness, but also as something which could be treated. In 1923 the Maudsley was able to admit civilian voluntary patients.

In Italy Cesare Lombroso, taking up the theories of Morel, went one step further, claiming that criminals and psychiatric patients were identifiable physically through their features. They were often evolutionary throwbacks, whose low brows and jutting jaws were to be found in non-European races and apes. In Germany, although asylums existed, the main body of knowledge was in the universities and medically–orientated research. Consequently a distinctive approach to psychiatry developed, in which the scientific understanding of psychiatric disorders was paramount.

In the nineteenth century the development of psychiatry took some quite strange twists and turns. 'Animal magnetism', hypnotism, played its part, mainly because it revealed new things about the mind and how it worked. It became widely used as a diagnostic tool. Freud, who received his MD in medicine and physiology in 1881, used hypnotism to treat hysterical symptoms by leading patients back to the beginning of each symptom. He developed his theory that neurosis in women patients resulted from early sexual trauma, or abuse, by the father. He later rejected this, turning heavily to the Oedipus complex as an explanation. Freud also moved away from hypnosis in favour of psychoanalysis, dream interpretation and free association as means of uncovering hidden unconscious wishes. His ideas, particularly the concept of the dynamic unconscious, had a deep influence on psychiatry and understanding of the mind. Freud, incidentally, harboured some very strange views about physically disabled people. He said they were 'malformed and maladjusted', and added that this was because of their denial of the 'reality factor'. He used Richard III as an illustration, arguing that he wreaked havoc on the world because of his disability, and that he thought life owed him reparation because of his congenital deformities. Freud concluded that disabled people showed their hostility towards society by trying to demand unfair privileges over others.

Some thought was now being given to after-care. The work of the Mental After-Care Association, started in 1879, had shown that after-care was not only possible but helpful. By 1918 it was dealing with 670 cases annually. Ex-patients were placed in convalescent homes for a time after their initial discharge, occasionally with families, and sometimes through friendship and individual voluntary help. By 1924 the Association was taking 'early' care, as well as after care, into its remit.

Psychoanalysis became widely used, particularly in the United States. It was less popular in Britain and took some years to become accepted as a method of treatment. Between the 'twenties' and 'forties' in Britain there was major colony building in large hospitals to house mentally disturbed people.

However, shock treatments for treating neuroses or psychoses had not disappeared. Insulin shock treatment was used for schizophrenia, and camphor produced such a response in epileptics that the resulting convulsions caused broken bones in some patients. In 1938 in Genoa, Ugo Cerletti was the first to use electric shocks to help with severe depression. Surgery was also tried: in Lisbon Egas Moniz used frontal leucotomy, the severance of the frontal lobes from the rest of the brain, in an attempt to overcome melancholic cases. Although he received a Nobel Prize for this work in 1949, he was greatly attacked for altering the mental states of the individuals on which he experimented.

The second half of the twentieth century heralded the era of psychotropic drugs. For the first time psychiatrists had tools which could control behaviour. The first of these drugs, Lithium, appeared in 1949 as a means of managing manic depression. This was quickly followed in the nineteen-fifties by antipsychotics and antidepressants, notably Largactil and Imipramine.

There was a new optimism abroad in psychiatry. These means of controlling behaviour chemically brought with them new thinking on asylums, and the first plans emerged of resettling the residents into the community, particularly into small, family-sized hostels in ordinary houses in ordinary streets and towns. It also brought new outlooks for psychiatry. No longer focussed completely on extreme cases in asylums, there was a growing re-alisation of the less acute, borderline problems of people in the community who needed help. The use of drugs to treat these milder cases became universal, and were often criticised for causing addiction. During the nineteen-sixties Librium and Valium were prescribed widely for anxiety states, particularly to women. In more recent years, the development of drugs, like the anti-depressant Prozac, have resulted from a more organic un-derstanding of what goes on in the brain.

Despite these improved treatments, there have been few cures of persistent mental conditions. Alzheimer's disease, which affects older people, continues to be one of the most stubborn and per-sistent takers of people's minds. In recent years high-profile cases, like former President Ronald Reagan and novelist Iris Murdoch, have led to greater public understanding and sympathy. Research, largely in the United States but also in Britain, much of it made possible through the efforts of the Alzheimer's Society, revolu-tionised in recent years by Harry Cayton, is bearing fruit. Key markers of the disease, the proteins cystatin C and beta 2 microglobulin, have been identified, which could make early diagnosis possible. Environmental factors which could be causative have been suggested, among them excessive aluminium in drinking water, smoking, poor diet and lack of exercise. Medication is now available to help minimise symptoms.

Alongside chemical and other therapeutic treatments of mental health problems, has been the growth of psychotherapy, bringing with it controversy, but the approval of hundreds of thousands of people who take part in group sessions, family therapy, and consciousness-raising. They are gentle techniques, if not fully understood, and a long way from the restraints of the manacles and iron bars of not so long ago. However, at the core of all this there is still a group of people for whom chemicals may provide some alleviation but for whom the problems still exist for themselves and their families. At the same time, the stigma attached to mental health problems is still in the air like a pungent smell that will not go away.

Chapter Eight

Mental Health Legislation

The first traceable mental health legislation is the De Prerogativa Regis of 1324 – 'The Royal Prerogative', – which provided for the management of estates of tenants who became incapable of doing so through illness. The Crown was entitled to take the rents and profits of the estates of 'idiots' for their lifetime, after the expense of their maintenance and that of any dependent family. The care of the idiot was usually entrusted to somebody who was responsible also for sharing the profits from the estate with the Crown. 'Lunatics' fared slightly better: any excess remaining after the cost of their care had been deducted was held in trust for them until they recovered, or if they died before recovery, 'for the benefit of their soul'.

On the whole, however, early legislation did not differentiate between paupers and the reasons for their poverty, or between mental disability, mental illness or social conditions. This was clear in the 1601 Act for the Relief of the Poor, which placed responsibility on parishes for the old and the sick, including 'idiots' and 'lunatics', and to provide work for them. The 'parish' usually meant that unpaid church wardens and others connected with churches took on the burden, often none too willingly. The parish had to find money for the relief of its own poor and disabled and to levy local rates. Relief was not obtained easily: the system was founded on work and punishment. Magistrates committed those paupers refusing to work to the common jail. Mentally disabled people fared badly: they were usually committed to the workhouses, where conditions were horrendous. Wayfarers, sane or insane, travelling through parishes were unpopular because they could seek relief. The Act of Settlement 1662 made it law that relief could be restricted to people belonging to the parish. Workhouses continued to become the dumping ground for these unfortunates, in reality for their punishment. The first seeds of 'certification' came in 1714. A new Act of Parliament unified the laws relating to rogues, vagabonds, sturdy beggars and vagrants into one piece of legislation. Under this Parliament gave authority to two or more magistrates to order the arrest of any person 'furiously mad and dangerous…to be safely locked up in some secure place', and to be kept there for as long as 'the lunacy or madness shall continue'. Lunatics were however given one concession: they were to receive the same treatment under the Act as other vagrants but were not to be whipped.

The growth in 'madhouses' led to dubious practices by which people made use of them to put eccentric, or even unwanted, relatives away and then to lay hands on their money and estates. This led in 1763 to a half-hearted investigation by Parliament into practices in London's madhouses, which in turn gave birth to the Act for Regulating Madhouses 1774. For the first time this introduced medical certification for the insane, though it merely provided for a £100 fine unless the proprietor of a private madhouse received when the patient was delivered to him 'an order, in writing under the hand and seal of some physician, surgeon or apothecary, that such person is proper to be received into such house or place as a lunatick'. It applied only to private patients, and meant that the pauper insane could still be confined by magistrates under the Act of 1774. It was the poor who most needed protection; they had no money, and were most likely to be neglected and ill-treated. Parishes paid a pittance for their keep out of which the madhouse proprietor still ensured he made a profit.

The 1774 Act did lead to a system of licensing and inspecting madhouses in the London area, but there was nothing in the legislation to empower the Commissioners to withdraw a licence on the grounds of conditions or ill-treatment of residents. In any case, the Commissioners managed to squeeze their inspections into just six days a year, and in that time visited around eight establishments a day. Conditions for the mentally disabled pauper remained horrific.

In 1800 an Act for the Safe Custody of Insane Persons Charged with Offences came about because of the unfortunate attempted assassination of George III by an ex-soldier, James Hadfield. At his trial it was accepted that Hadfield was suffering from brain damage following a head injury. The Act allowed courts to pass a verdict of not guilty by reason of insanity, and for people sentenced in this way to be detained at His Majesty's pleasure.

In 1808 Sir George Onesiphoris Paul initiated a campaign which led to the County Asylum Act of 1808 and the first institutions built and specifically designed for 'criminal and pauper lunatics'. Counties were allowed to raise rates to build them, but the response was poor. Even by 1842 only 17 asylums had been built in just 15 counties. Five of these had more than the recommended 200 patients: Kent, built in 1833 with 300 patients; Surrey, built in 1841 had 360 patients; Wakefield, built 1818, 420 patients; Lancaster's, built 1816, 611 patients; and Hanwell, built 1831, 975 patients. There were asylums built at Nottingham in 1812; Norfolk in 1814; Staffordshire in 1818; Lincoln in 1820; Cornwall in 1820; Gloucester in 1823; Suffolk in 1829; Chester in 1829; Dorset in 1832; Leicestershire in 1837; Shropshire and Montgomery in 1845; Devon in 1845; and Oxfordshire and Berkshire in 1846. Goodness knows what lunatics and idiots did for accommodation in other areas, where it appeared that no provision was made. In truth, like in all areas whether they possessed an asylum or not, many of them were still in prisons and workhouses.

Following scandals and investigations at Bedlam and the York

Asylum in 1815, a Parliamentary Select Committee was set-up to inquire into conditions in madhouses and charitable asylums. They published findings showing that beatings and whippings were common punishments and that prolonged restraint was used routinely to manage inmates. They made recommendations that a system of asylums at public expense should be provided, and that there should be a vigorous system of independent inspection. At about the same time, the Care and Maintenance of Lunatics Act 1815 made it compulsory for overseers of the poor to produce lists of lunatics and idiots in parishes and to send the lists to Parliament with certificates from medical practitioners.

For three years between 1816 and 1819 members of the Select Committee presented three Bills aimed at establishing a permanent commission to be appointed by the Home Office to inspect and enforce standards of conduct and treatment in private madhouses. None succeeded in reaching the statute book, although parliamentary concern persisted. Following reports about abuse and neglect of patients of the White House Madhouse in the County of Middlesex, another Select Committee on Pauper Lunatics and Lunatic Asylums was appointed and started work in 1827. They found that because there were only two paid attendants at the White House for 164 inmates, patients had to do all the work. Moreover, so that the two attendants could have some free time over weekends, patients were chained into cribs at three o'clock on Saturday afternoon and remained there until Monday morning.

Lord Ashley was appointed to the Metropolitan Commission in Lunacy in 1828, and it proved a good day for reformers. He was later to become the 7th Earl of Shaftesbury, a man of strong social conscience, who initiated reform in other areas, particularly the workplace, and to benefit the climbing boys and children in the Ragged Schools. What he witnessed in his role on the Commission led him to campaign for mental health reform, and to the passing of the Madhouse Act 1828. This repealed the 1774 Act and, as his colleagues had demanded a decade earlier, increased the number of Metropolitan Commissioners to fifteen.

They could now recommend that a private madhouse's licence be revoked if conditions were poor, and require the release of any patient they considered to be improperly confined. The Act also made it compulsory for a doctor to visit inmates at least once a week and to sign a weekly register, and if there were over 100 patients there had to be a doctor in the establishment itself. Unfortunately these provisions applied only to private madhouses, and not to county and charitable asylums. Two magistrates, or the overseer of the poor and one vicar, had the power to certify pauper lunatics and idiots; but the order had to be accompanied by a medical certificate.

The County Asylums Act 1828 required that magistrates send annual returns on admissions, discharges and deaths to the Home Office. Over a decade later, legislation ended the stipulation in the Poor Law Amendment Act 1834 that paupers had to go into a workhouse to gain parish relief. It also restricted the detention of any dangerous lunatic, insane person or idiot in any workhouse to the maximum of fourteen days. This meant in practice that the dangerous lunatic was passed on to a county asylum, and that workhouses cared for the non-dangerous lunatic. Even so, there appears to have been little change in treatment: John Conolly, one of the most famous of the madhouse doctors, when visiting asylums in 1839, found various devices of leather and iron, straitjackets and hand and leg irons.

The Insane Prisoners Act 1840 merely gave the Home Secretary the power to take from a prison to an asylum any person awaiting trial or serving a sentence on the basis of a certificate signed by two magistrates and two doctors. This was followed quickly by the Care and Treatment of Lunatics and Lunatic Asylums Inspection Act 1842, which extended the power of the Commissioners to England and Wales as a whole. They were then renamed the Commissioners in Lunacy by the Care and Treatment of Lunatics Act 1845.

The 1845 Act, pioneered largely by Lord Ashley, was landmark legislation. Before its enactment there was no single code for the treatment of the insane. Ashley had long pressed for legal control over private madhouses, and this was achieved by the 1845 Act. A more detailed form of certification was introduced which stepped-up the safeguards against wrongful detention for private patient and pauper insane alike. Those who signed the certificate for admission could also sign for a patient's discharge. All asylums had to keep records of doctor's visits and the treatment received by each patient. The County Asylums Act, passed in the same year, made it compulsory for every county and borough to provide within three years, adequate places at public expense for its poor lunatics.

After the 1845 Act public attention became preoccupied less by the treatment of the insane than by detention of the sane in asylums. Previously there had been much illegal detention to get sick relatives certified as a way of gaining their possessions. They were then kept against their will, banned from writing to or making contact with anybody in the outside world. The madhouse keepers were able to charge high fees for the 'patient's' care, and there was little chance of their ever seeing life outside the asylum again. Sometimes the names of these unfortunate detainees were changed so that they disappeared. Even after the 1845 Act there was much public concern that illegal imprisonment for gain was continuing. The Alleged Lunatics' Friends Society was set up by Luke James Hansard, son of the original printer of the House of Commons, 'for the protection of the British subject from unjust confinement on the grounds of mental derangement, and for the redress of persons so confined'. This group's campaigning, much resented by the doctors working in the asylums, led to three amending Acts passed in 1853. The first concerned itself with private asylums and provided for closer inspection of the certification of their patients. The second was about provision in public asylums and how people were admitted to them. The third covered the Chancery lunatics, those whose cases, under an Act of Parliament in the reign of Edward II, had to come before a jury when relatives petitioned for the 'insane' person to be certified to prevent him dissipating a family fortune. These were very minor measures that did not satisfy the Alleged

Lunatics' Friends Society which continued to campaign. The 1853 Act also required the medical officer to write in the medical notes of patients whether patients were restrained, by what method, for how long and the reasons for it.

The Alleged Lunatics' Friends Society achieved more satisfaction when in 1859, under the second Derby administration, a Select Committee was appointed to look at the issue of certification and the care of the insane. Its report published a year later recommended that a magistrate's order should be obtained in cases of private certification, but many Parliamentarians, including Shaftesbury, opposed this because, they said, it delayed treatment. A year later the Criminal Lunatics Asylums Act 1860 established the Broadmoor centre for the criminally insane, controlled specifically by the Home Office.

There was still, however, widespread public attention on the dangers of sane people being put into asylums, but far fewer concerns about improving the treatment of those confined in asylums. This was added to by publicity given to the case of Mrs.Georgiana Weldon, an eccentric woman, who fought long and hard through the courts and publicly in the press to ward off an order by her husband to have her certified. After suing practically everybody in sight, including two doctors who signed the certification order, Mrs.Weldon managed to keep out of the asylum. Baron Huddleston's summing up fuelled public opinion: 'It is somewhat startling – it is positively shocking – that if a pauper, or as Mrs.Weldon put it, a crossing-sweeper should sign an order, and another crossing-sweeper should make a statement, and then that two medical men, who had never had a day's practice in their lives, should for a small sum of money grant their certificates, a person may be lodged in a private lunatic asylum, and that this order, and the statement and these certificates are a perfect answer to any action.'

The case led to demands for a change in the laws relating to mental health. The Lord Chancellor, Lord Selborne, led the charge. He had previously shown a strong personal interest, having in 1883 introduced a Lunacy Bill in the House of Lords which had been withdrawn because of lack of support. Lord Milltown a year later put forward a motion that 'in the opinion of this House, the existing state of the Lunacy Laws is unsatisfactory, and constitutes a serious danger to the liberty of the subject'. He made reference to the judgement in the Weldon case, which had just been reported, 'that a person could be confined in an asylum by anybody, on the statement of anybody, provided certain formalities were gone through'. In 1885 Selborne introduced a Lunacy Amendment Bill, but it was shelved. Two years later two Bills were introduced by Lord Halsbury. The first drew existing legislation together and made it more coherent. The second was the Lunacy Laws Amendment Bill, which brought forward again a clause requiring a magistrate's order in non-pauper cases of insanity.

When this clause was opposed by the Lunacy Commissioners under a plea that it would delay early treatment, a compromise was reached that a magistrate's order would not be needed in every case, but that the person alleged to be insane had the right to demand the presence of a Justice if he or she wished to defend the action. Both Bills got through the Lords and went on to the Commons. The first survived through to a third reading, but the Amendment Bill was withdrawn by the Solicitor-General after its first reading. In consequence both Bills failed to become Acts, because Selborne would not allow one Bill to go forward without the other.

The Lord Chancellor again tried to introduce the Lunacy Acts Amendment Bill in 1888, but it failed in the Commons. He persisted, and a year later introduced the Bill for a third time. By then most parliamentarians were tired of the whole subject, and it passed wearily into law as the Lunacy Act 1890. This was long, complicated and appeared to cover every possible safeguard against a sane person being put away. It proved so cumbersome and restrictive that it handicapped progress towards early medical and social treatment for many years.

One of its greatest failings was that it still made no distinction between the insane and the mentally defective. It defined lunatic as 'an idiot or person of unsound mind', although by then many in the field were recognising mental deficiency as a separate condition. Work and research undertaken in France earlier in the nineteenth century had recognised the difference and made the case that those who were mentally deficient could be trained in such a way that the effects of the condition were minimised. This had begun to win acceptance in Britain from the mid-nineteenth century, and several schools for idiots appeared. By 1881 the classification of mental deficiency as a separate classification was receiving such wide recognition that a survey was made - called 'a return of idiots' – which concluded that there were 29,452 in public institutions – workhouses, lunatic asylums and prisons – but that only some 3% were in places specifically designed for their training. Indeed, agitation by the Charity Organisation Society resulted in a very conservative Idiots Bill being introduced into Parliament which became the Idiots Act 1886.

This defined 'an idiot or imbecile from birth or from an early age' and allowed local authorities to establish institutions for idiots, with a medical certificate and a statement from a parent or guardian as the means of entry. Although the Act specifically determined that the terms idiot and imbecile did not include lunatics, the Lunacy Act 1890 still managed not to include any distinction. This meant a struggle would be needed, including separate legislation, in years to come to gain provision for mentally deficient people. It was not until the Mental Deficiency Act 1913 – defined as applying to idiots, imbeciles, feeble-minded persons and moral defectives and applying only to those whose normal development had been arrested in childhood by illness or brain injury – that any real expansion and development in provision became possible. This was followed in 1927 by a further Act which amended that of 1913, and added training to the responsibilities of supervision and protection.

In Britain the First World War limited the possibility of any legislative change. A Bill 'to facilitate the early treatment of mental disorder of recent origin' through voluntary admission to asylums was put before the Commons by Cecil Harmsworth in

1915, but it was withdrawn after its second reading because there was what Parliament saw as more urgent business. Under the 1890 Lunacy Act it had become possible for voluntary patients to go into private – not public – asylums without certification for early treatment. Harmsworth's Bill sought to extend this to public asylums and after the war the Board of Control adopted his ideas in a report it placed before the Government Reconstruction Committee. The report recommended the extension of voluntary treatment, a narrowing of the gap between the way mental and physical illness was treated, the development of out-patient clinics and after-care, and improvement of professional standards in psychiatry. Here was a blueprint for the reform of mental health care in Britain, but it was a time of extreme financial stringency in local Government and by 1921 plans for improvement had been shelved.

One measure that did help was the establishment in 1919 of the Ministry of Health, under the Ministry of Health Act of that year. It inherited all the powers and functions of the Local Government Board and within a year had also taken over responsibility for lunacy and mental deficiency, including the Board of Control. However, public faith in asylums remained low. Their reputation was not helped by a book published just after the war called *The Experience of an Asylum Doctor* by Dr Montague Lomax who worked in Prestwich Hospital in Manchester. He claimed that inmates were cruelly treated, badly fed and clothed, that they were closely confined, and the staff largely unqualified. So great was the impact of the book that the Minister of Health appointed a Committee of Enquiry. This came to the conclusion that, although conditions at Prestwich were far from satisfactory, what Dr Lomax had found was in large part due to the war when there was understaffing and qualified people were away serving in the forces. The committee was also asked to consider conditions in other asylums, but was handicapped by not having the power to hear witnesses on oath and was thus unable to protect early whistle-blowers from victimisation.

The consequences of their report were almost exclusively

confined to structural issues and staff conditions. They recommended a halt to the building of large, barren asylums, and that they should be replaced by smaller institutions of one thousand beds made up of a number of smaller units. They also criticised the lack of suitable trained staff to work in asylums.

Despite these changes in focus, the public mind could still not rid itself of the belief that the real problem with asylums was the risk of sane people being placed in them by mistake. Indeed, in 1924 the Board of Control gave its reason for initiating a Royal Commission on Lunacy and Mental Disorder as 'uneasiness aroused in the public mind by a number of charges, somewhat recklessly made, to the effect that large numbers of sane persons were being detained as insane, that the whole system of lunacy administration was wrong, and that widespread cruelty existed in our public mental hospitals'. Whatever the reasons for a Royal Commission, its findings were to establish officially for the first time actions on early and after care – care in the community. It recommended the lunacy laws should be revised to ensure that the treatment of mental disorders should compare as nearly as possible with the treatment of physical illnesses, and that certification should be a last resort, not a preliminary to treatment. There should also be no distinction in the method of certification used for private and pauper patients. Voluntary patients should be able to go into mental hospitals without legal measures and to leave on giving 72 hours' notice. Local authorities should be encouraged to setup out-patient clinics, to create observation beds and after care. Mental hospitals should not exceed 1,000 beds, and should be designed on a villa system. Employment and entertainment for patients should be developed, and a person should be appointed in every hospital to organise the work of social rehabilitation.

The Royal Commission's Report at last demonstrated that the legalistic straight jacket created by the 1890 Act was giving way to a humane medical view and the development of ideas on after-care and rehabilitation. The Board of Control clamoured for parliamentary action on the Commission's findings: 'It is regrettable that the poorer classes should be denied facilities for the treatments which are open to those more fortunately circumstanced.'

The Board had its wishes granted in 1930 with the passing of the Mental Treatment Act. Its main contribution to improvement in mental health care was that it made possible voluntary treatment, and that it encouraged the establishment of both psychiatric outpatient clinics and observation wards. It also brought in welcome changes in language. The Local Government Act of 1929 had already eliminated terms such as pauper and poor law, and now asylum was replaced by hospital, lunatic replaced by patient or person of unsound mind.

As always it took many years for the encouragement the Act gave to translate into effective action, especially in respect of good outpatient clinics and the treatment of psychoneurosis. In the mental hospitals there were welcome changes like the introduction of occupational therapy, more and better trained staff, and in a range of smaller improvements, like that covering which personal possessions patients were able to keep, such as hairbrushes and combs.

In mental deficiency services there was little adequate development: there remained a lack of specialist schools and care generally. The main problem was that there was still no central body with the power to enforce overall standards and levels of care nationwide. Some local authorities developed good services, but others were failing dismally, particularly in terms of community care. The Second World War did nothing to improve the situation, with many doctors and nurses called away for service, and some mental hospitals taken over for military use. It was only after the war, with the birth of the National Health Service, that a unified approach was achieved.

The mental hospitals, like all other hospitals, came under the authority of the new Regional Hospital Boards, whilst local authorities were given the responsibility of prevention, care and after-care of illness and mental defectiveness. The Ministry of Health became the central authority for mental health. Under a system of national standards and guidance the period from 1948 saw the beginnings of a real community service in mental health. It witnessed the development of home visits, after-care, out-patient clinics, half-way houses, as well as concepts like day hospitals and night hospitals. This could be seen as progress but in terms of legislation there had been no fundamental revision of the law relating to mental health since the 1890 Lunacy Act. Measures like the 1930 Mental Treatment Act and the Mental Deficiency Acts from 1913 through to 1927 had brought changes in treatment but the code still remained intact. In fact, there had been no full parliamentary debate on mental health since 1930. This was rectified in February 1954 when a debate was initiated by Labour MP Kenneth Robinson, who two years earlier had become the chairman of the North-West Metropolitan Hospitals Board's mental health committee, on the motion: 'That this House, whilst recognising the advances made in recent years in the treatment and care of mental patients, expresses its concern at the serious overcrowding of mental hospitals and mental deficiency hospitals, and at the acute shortage of nursing and junior medical staff in the Mental Health Service; and calls upon HM Government and the hospital authorities to make adequate provision for the modernisation and development of this essential service.'

The Royal Commission which followed the debate took evidence for three years. Its main recommendations were: that the description 'mental disorder' should be used to cover all forms of mental ill-health, and that this would include three main categories, mentally ill patients, psychopathic patients, and severely subnormal patients; that patients should be admitted to mental hospitals and mentally deficiency hospitals as to other types of hospital; and that certification, now to be termed compulsory detention, should be used only where treatment was considered urgently necessary. New regional bodies should perform the duties of investigating wrongful detention, taking over this role from the Board of Control.

The subsequent 1959 Mental Health Act repealed all previous legislation. Because it set out to tidy-up, simplify and amend all previous law on the subject, it became a long and complex document. It provided a single code for all types of mental disorder, but perhaps its most important achievement was in Section 5 which brought greater freedom for mental health patients. Under this they could be admitted to any hospital without formalities of any kind and without liability to detention. The 1959 Act also hugely extended the freedom of patients whilst in hospital, in dramatic contrast to conditions a century before when, once patients were certified, they were not allowed to write letters or have contact with anybody in the world outside without specific permission and censorship. Now, they would be provided with pocket money for personal expenses, there were no restrictions on correspondence for those informally admitted, and letters addressed to MPs, the Health Minister, or a member of a Mental Health Review Tribunal had to be forwarded in all cases. Only letters written by patients liable to compulsory detention were supervised.

The Act set up regional mental health review tribunals which took over the safeguarding functions of the Board of Control. They were required to review cases of compulsory detention when asked by patients or their relatives. The Act also provided for an application for admission to be made by a mental welfare officer or the patient's nearest relative:

- For observation – up to twenty-eight days, two medical certificates, not renewable. If there is a need for further detention, the patient will have to be reassessed for admission.

- In an emergency – up to seventy-two hours, one medical certificate, which may be converted, by the addition of a further medical certificate, into an order for observation.

- For treatment – up to twelve months in the first instance, two medical certificates, renewable for twelve months and thereafter for periods of two years. A Mental Health Review Tribunal hearing can be applied for, once in the first period of detention and once in each period for which detention is renewed.

There was general acknowledgement that community care was not however keeping pace with these changes in hospital care. The Seebolm Report in 1968 said that community care of the mentally disordered was, in many parts of the country, 'still a sad illusion, and judging by the published plans, will remain so for years ahead'.

The Mental Health (Amendment) Act 1983 heralded the Mental Health Act 1983. which, while continuing the trends set in the 1959 Act by further encouraging informal admissions, also appeared to take a more legalistic approach. It set more limits on the exercise of legal powers and also established statutory rights to after-care.

In the 1990's a number of high profile incidents in which discharged mental health patients were involved, brought public clamour for a more legalistic approach to certification and discharge. In December 1992, a man suffering from schizophrenia, attacked and killed Jonathan Zito at a London tube station. This led to the Mental Health (Patients in the Community) Act 1995, providing for more strictly supervised discharge and supervision of after-care patients.

In 1998, Professor Genevra Richardson was appointed by the Government to carry out a review of the 1983 Mental Health Act. The report was published in November 1999, together with a Green Paper entitled *Reform of the Mental Health Act – Proposals for Consultation*. Its emphasis was on offering informal care, the provision of the least restrictive alternative compatible with the delivery of safe and effective care, consensual care, reciprocity, respect for diversity and the recognition of the role of carers. 'The Committee is convinced that if society is to impose a duty to comply with care and treatment on some of those who suffer from mental disorder it must impose a parallel duty on health and social care authorities to provide an appropriate standard of care and treatment for those subject to compulsion.'

In December 2000 the White Paper *Reforming the Mental Health Act* appeared, and in June 2002 a draft Mental Health Bill was published and circulated for a twelve month period of consultation.

Despite Professor Richardson's statements on informal care, the draft Bill caused great controversy because under it many people with mental disorders considered to be dangerous, but who have not committed any dangerous act or crime, could be detained in secure accommodation indefinitely. It also allowed the compulsory treatment of mentally ill people in the community by forcing them to take medicines in clinics. Critics argue that this is a return to the restrictive code of the 1890 Act, and a breach of human rights, because judgements will have to be made about what people might do, rather than making judgements based on what people have already done. Treating people against their will is also being questioned. The draft Bill's supporters pointed out that under its proposals no-one would be detained for longer than 28 days without an independent examination, which would also determine the length of treatment.

At the time of writing, the Bill is still before Parliament.

Chapter Nine

Aktion T4 – The Nazi 'Euthanasia' Programme for Disabled Children and Adults

There has been no harsher illustration, before or since, of the effect social attitudes can inflict on disabled people than that provided by the German Aktion T4 programme just before and during World War II, which led to the mass killing of disabled children and adults purely on grounds of economy and cleaning up genetic lineages. Using the mask of 'euthanasia', Hitler eliminated over 70,000 disabled people, mostly mental health patients. The disabled children were killed first because this was considered easier and would provide a pilot for the more difficult task of eliminating the adults.

However, the instigators of the 'euthanasia' programme, the Nazis, may not have given birth to this satanic conception. Most people know of the unspeakable Dr Mengele's Auschwitz experiments, but research since then has brought to light the involvement of many others in the medical profession in developing Nazi policy, more particularly in exterminating those whose 'lives were unworthy of life' – disabled people. As early as 1895, Adolf Jost, in his book *The Right to Death* (Das Recht auf den Tod) advocated medical killings on the grounds that control over the death of the individual must belong to the state if this social organism was to control its own health. There are also indications that, long before the Nazis came to power, the views of parents of institutionalised mentally and physically disabled people played a part in justifying – or at least providing the excuse for – the 'euthanasia' policies which were to follow.

After World War I, German psychiatry was obsessed with the balance between reform of treatment and the economic cost of keeping in an institution people with a mental disability. Under the Nazis, eugenic arguments came to dominate the social scene, together with even greater emphasis on the need for savings in the cost of treatment.

It was a German psychiatrist, Professor Alfred Hoche, of the University of Freiburg, together with lawyer Professor Karl Binding, of the University of Leipzig, who in 1920 coined the phrase 'life unworthy of life'. In a book – *The Permission to Destroy Life Unworthy of Life* (Die Freigabe der Vernichtung Lebensunwerten Leben) they questioned whether a country facing dire economic crisis immediately after World War I could afford to support and treat a growing number of 'mental defectives'. They argued that the non-consensual killing of 'idiots' and the mentally ill and other 'entirely unproductive persons' would be a sacrifice worth making for the sake of the economic health of the nation. Hoche described the intended disabled victims as 'empty shells of human beings'. Binding laid out the jurisdiction by which this euthanasia could be safely achieved, and Hoche dealt with the medical ethics and methods. Incredibly now, they actually described what they were advocating as 'purely a healing treatment'.

There were some critics of those who advocated euthanasia. In 1925 Ewald Meltzer, who directed the work of the Katherinenhof Asylum at Grosshennersdorf in Saxony, wrote a critique of Binding and Hoche, which recounted the happiness that disabled people found in life, despite their problems. However, Meltzer unwittingly helped further the arguments for a state euthanasia programme. When he sought the views on euthanasia held by the fathers and mothers of the youngsters in his institution, he was surprised to discover that nearly three-quarters of the 162 parents who answered his questionnaire would favour the 'painless curtailment of the life of their child if experts established that he or she was suffering from incurable idiocy'.

Moreover, less than a half of the parents who rejected the concept of euthanasia did so completely: twenty-three of them consented to their child being killed in the event of their own death and the child becoming an orphan. Subsequently when the Nazis came to power, the results of Melzer's survey were quoted by them equally as much as the arguments of Binding and Hoche.

Later, in the 1930s, other medical professionals were suggesting the eradication of this "burden" on the nation's resources. Also in the interest of long-term cost cutting and national purity, on 14th July 1933 came the Law for the Prevention of Hereditarily Diseased Progeny, which brought in compulsory sterilisation for those with hereditary illnesses. It provided the legal framework under which some 300,000 disabled people were sterilized. Although those sterilised were classified as mental patients, they included many disabled people who were not – epileptics, the blind, prelingually deaf people, the senile, people with physical abnormalities, and alcoholics. The new law necessitated setting up 220 local Hereditary Health Courts which made decisions about who should be sterilised. Before cases reached these courts, psychiatrists were among those made statutorily responsible for initiating the procedures and often sat in the courts themselves.

School teachers were also asked to encourage pupils to construct family trees so that defective relatives could be identified and referred to the court.

The relentless propaganda to justify such policies contained references to the burden placed by asylums and disabled people in general upon the wealth and health of the population. In films disabled people were pinpointed as a threat to the 'hereditary health of the racial collective'. The language used was horrific, at once unscientific and irresponsible. It questioned whether those so targeted were still humans, and used descriptions like 'creatures' and 'beings' and went on to associate insanity with sex-offenders and murderers.

The Hereditary Health Courts did not restrict themselves to dealing only with those who appeared before them. Psychiatrist Hermann Pfannmuller, who was a judge in the court at Kempten, decided that a young woman who appeared before him should be sterilised. Not content with this he went out and found twenty-one other members of her family. He subsequently ordered the sterilisation of ten of these 'degenerates' because 'the danger of reproduction appeared imminent'. Nor were courts at all fussy about their classifications of hereditary disability: alcoholics, reformed alcoholics and people with low alcohol tolerance who imbibed only small amounts of alcohol were sterilized as 'chronic alcoholics'. The excuse was that alcoholism pointed to some psychopathic or asocial disorder. There were strong indications that many in the psychiatric profession were attracted both to sterilisation and euthanasia as a means of eliminating people whose very existence tended to underline how little they were able to do to help them.

Building on the sterilisation of disabled and handicapped people made possible by enacted legislation in 1933, some began to take up Hoche and Binding's ideas for a programme of 'mercy killing'. In August of that year, Professor Walter Schultze, Commissioner for Health in Bavaria, was bold enough to say that sterilisation was not enough and that the mentally retarded, psychopaths and other 'inferior persons' should be put to death. Of course, these attitudes rubbed off on the treatment people received in institutions. Mental hospitals were encouraged, by reducing their funding and ceasing to inspect them, to neglect those in their care. At the same time 'courses' were organised for Government officials in the hospitals, featuring the most outrageous behaviour of retarded and violent patients, as a means of preparing the participants for a programme of mercy killing. These courses were later extended to the press, the SS, party officials, the police and prison officials. By 1937 even the more liberal Meltzer had shifted his ground. He admitted to himself and the world at large that in a national emergency in which there was a shortage of food or in which beds were required for the wounded, 'the patient must pay his dues to the Fatherland through some form of involuntary mercy killing'.

The first recorded note of Hitler's intentions to rid the nation of the incurably ill through a programme of euthanasia came at the Nuremberg Party rally in 1935. It is recorded that his view was that a war needed a nation to be healthy, and that the lessened sense of the value of human life during a war made it easier to eliminate the incurably ill.

In 1938 Hitler took the final goose step and authorized the killing of handicapped infants. The programme avoided the usual legal and 'official' channels and was initiated directly from Hitler's headquarters at Tiergartenstrasse 4 in Berlin. It was no coincidence that the job was given to the Führer's own Chancellery, which was already responsible for dealing with petitions for mercy killings from the general population. This also meant that the Aktion T4 agency could act secretly and quietly outside Government.

The programme started with just one child named Knauer, born blind, without one leg and part of an arm, and said to be mentally retarded. The child's parents had petitioned the Government to the effect that their child should be allowed to die. Hitler sent Karl Brandt, his personal physician, to the clinic at the University of Leipzig to see the doctor caring for the child. Brandt had instructions to inform him that he could undertake the mercy killing of the child and that Hitler would see to it that there would be no legal consequences. When Brandt returned to Berlin, Hitler authorised Brandt to proceed in the same way in other cases.

Hitler gave Brandt the help of Philip Bouhler to establish the mechanisms of a euthanasia programme. Bouhler handed down the detailed execution of the undertaking to Viktor Brack, bureau chief in the Kanzlei des Führers, KdF. During the Spring of 1939, a KdF team developed plans for an efficient killing system. They began with newborn children, next with children up to three, then four, and then upwards. They issued a directive to identify victims, signed up physicians, set-up extermination sites in a number of hospitals, and established a front organisation, known as the Reich Committee for the Scientific Registration of Serious Hereditary and Congenital Diseases. This body then issued an order that it was to be informed of all children under three years of age in whom serious hereditary diseases were suspected. These included mental retardation, mongolism, malformations of all kinds, microcephaly and hydrocephaly. Even midwives had to file reports on newborn children.

The reports were in the form of a questionnaire. By June 1940 the content of the questionnaires had become denser: it included not only questions about illnesses and conditions, but now many on family histories of hereditary tendencies and excessive use of alcohol, tobacco and drugs. Three 'experts' in Berlin, without physically seeing or examining the child, then made a judgement. Each of the three came to an individual decision: if he or she decided that 'treatment' should be given – in other words extermination – a plus sign was written. The children recommended for extermination were sent to institutions with names like Children's Specialty Departments or Therapeutic Convalescent Institutions. In fact, there were no such establishments: the children were scattered among other young patients, but a few were kept in separate wards. Some thirty mercy killing zones were set up within existing institutions in Germany, Austria and Poland.

To persuade parents, they were promised that their children would receive revolutionary new treatments, but the doctors added that this entailed serious risks. Faced with no prospect whatever of being offered anything else that would help, they usually consented. The children were kept alive for a number of weeks to create the impression that some form of treatment was being administered. Killing was usually achieved through tablets dissolved in liquid over a period of time until the children lapsed into unconsciousness and finally death. Where the child could not drink, injections were used. However, there was also some experimentation with a technique of starvation to save the cost of medication. This was undertaken by Dr Hermann Pfannmuller at the Eglfing-Haar institution. As time went by, the age of the children within the programme increased and eventually adolescents, including juvenile delinquents, were included. Some 6,000 sick and disabled children and adolescents were killed through this early programme.

Much later in 1939 Hitler extended the policy of mass killing to include handicapped adults. He first made Leonardo Conti of RMdI responsible for implementation, but then decided to use the front organisation already established for children and gave the task of wider elimination to Brandt and Bouhler, who again handed it over to Brack. Since the front organisation was already there for the children, it did not take long to put in place an efficient killing machine. The front organisation was again established at Tiergarten Strasse 4, where at first euthanasia was achieved through back-door methods, quietly but with ruthless efficiency.

The Führer's authorisation of an adult euthanasia programme was given the label of an economy measure. Emergency beds and places were needed for those of German origin now streaming back from Russia and other parts of eastern Europe. It was done in the usual cold, calculated and methodical manner. The Führer's decree of October 1939 read: 'Reich Leader Bouhler and Dr Brandt are charged with the responsibility for expanding the authority of physicians, to be designated by name, to the end that patients considered incurable according to the best available human judgement of their state of health, can be granted a mercy death.'

It was written on Hitler's private letterhead and not as an official instrument of the state. And because it was felt that the German public was not yet quite ready to be told officially of the euthanasia policy, those appointed to administer actual killing were chosen carefully. Among them were several doctors already involved in the children's programme and others who were known to hold positive views about euthanasia. They were told that although there was no official law involved, the Führer's decree was the equivalent of law, and that he would ensure they were in no danger of prosecution. A 'front' organisation, the Reich Work Group of Sanitoriums and Nursing Homes, was created. At Tiergartenstrasse 4 a hidden bureaucracy was created which proceeded to register and select for extermination 70,000 people, among them epileptics, long-stay patients of all kinds, and schizophrenics. The forms used to bring suitable T4 candidates to light particularly asked about patients' ability to work, whether their conditions were terminal, whether they had been in the institutions for five years or more, whether they were considered criminally insane, and for details of their racial background.

They then chose the asylums which would serve as centres of extermination and transferred their victims to them. The SS selected teams of men they judged to be suitable to undertake mass murder and these were sent to six killing centres at Brandenburg, Grafeneck, Hartheim, Bernburg, Sonnenstein and Hadamar. Starting with an early trial run at Brandenburg in January 1940, the process of killing soon reached its peak and remained there until August 1941. Again doctors were carefully selected. They were briefed in Berlin before being sent first to observe the process and then to take part themselves. In eastern areas of the country, methods were less subtle: SS units were instructed to shoot psychiatric patients out of hand.

The administration was simple but efficient. Registration forms on every psychiatric patient were sent to assessors. Low productivity of whatever work they did within the asylum, incurable sickness, and the length of their stay in the institution were factors taken into account. The assessors were sent batches of two to three hundred forms, and were paid according to the number of assessments they made. One psychiatrist, Dr Josef Schreck, managed to make 15,000 assessments in a month. As soon as assessments had been made most victims were taken to a killing centre or, merely to relieve strain on the centres, to nearby asylums from which it was easy to transport them when there was less pressure on the killing centres.

There was a front organisation for the transportation of the doomed patients, called the Common Welfare Ambulance

Services. This ensured that not only the patients but their notes and a list of their personal possessions arrived as well. In fact, the SS staffed the buses, usually wearing the obligatory white coats so that they looked like medical personnel. The routes of the buses were kept strictly secret, even from the medical staff at the institutions they left. In order to increase this secrecy, the initial plan of sending patients direct to the killing centre was soon discontinued in favour of first sending them to observation or transit institutions where they stayed briefly before going on to their fates. The whole process made it impossible for relatives to trace them. Families were initially sent letters telling them that their loved one had to be transferred for secret, war-related matters.

When the time came for the final transfer to the killing centre, another communication informed them without, of course, revealing its location, adding that war reasons and shortage of staff made the arrangement of visits or contact with them impossible. Weeks later a third letter notified them of the death. Cause of death was faked. In fact, the death usually took place within a day of arrival and very little of the medical model of 'euthanasia' was observed. The six main killing centres employed carbon monoxide gas as the prefered mechanism, following on experiments undertaken at the former prison, Brandenburg. The results of using this method were compared with the use of injecting cyanide, morphine, scopolomine and curare. Dr Karl Brandt, himself in charge of the experiment, observed that those injected died slowly, in contrast to those who met their demise by the gas. The gas chamber, as at Auschwitz, was constructed like a shower room, with the gas being administered into water pipes with small holes through which the carbon monoxide was pumped . The SS man making the observations noted that the people in the chamber very soon collapsed 'without scenes or commotion'. Special stretchers, like conveyor belts, were used to move the bodies into ovens.

Although using gas destroyed any illusion of a 'medical' process, it was decided that it would not only be quicker but more 'humane'. When physicians put their dilemma before Hitler himself, the Führer is said to have asked what was the most humane method; and to maintain the appearance that it was a medical decision, a doctor was always present when the killings took place. Some corpses were set aside for dissection, but most were cremated.

The doctors were even issued guidelines on the type of causes of death that were plausible for the false death certificates. The illusion of medical practice was further maintained by sending relatives an urn containing any old ashes scraped up from the crematorium floor, together with a note to the effect that immediate cremation had been necessary for health reasons.

Any pretence of medical practice was thrust aside elsewhere. As Germany invaded other countries in their advance eastwards, the SS simply shot patients in mental institutions because their accommodation was needed for military personnel. There was a well recorded episode in Stralsund on the Baltic sea, where the bodies were buried by Polish prisoners who were then shot themselves. Other such incidents took place at Chelm-Lubielski in Poland and many in Russia. However, because the shootings caused trauma in soldiers involved, gassing like that used in Germany itself was introduced, this time using mobile gas chambers. In a period of two weeks in the summer of 1940, over fifteen hundred mental patients were gassed in vans at a camp in Soldau.

Under the Aktion T4 programme, Jewish patients were soon subjected to different treatment. They did not have to meet the ordinary definitions – mental deficiency or mental problem, length of stay in hospital, ability to work and so on – they just had to be a patient and Jewish. In April 1940 the Reich Interior Ministry issued an order that an inventory was to be provided of all Jewish patients within three weeks whatever their condition. In June, 200 Jews, among them children, died in the Brandenburg killing centre. Others quickly followed in July and August. They always went to their deaths as Jewish groups because, in the words of one Nazi official, 'Aryan mental patients could not be expected to die together with Jewish patients…'.

It was, in fact, the precursor of the final solution. Later in 1940 Jewish patients began to be taken to Poland as part of the strategy of ridding Germany of Jews.

Sadly, many asylums, some of them run by Christian organisations, must have helped their patients on their way to their gruesome fate. Fifty percent of those killed under the Aktion T4 came from institutions under the management of the Protestant Inner Mission and the Roman Catholic Caritas Association. This was not wholly surprising since at least one of the medical directors of these Christian asylums had as early as 1937 been bold enough to say publicly that idiots were a travesty of mankind and should be returned to the Creator as soon as possible. Some Inner Mission asylums became holding centres for patients, and Protestant sisters staffed the Bernburg asylum during the time that 20,000 patients were killed on their premises. Some psychiatrists did their best to slow down the euthanasia process by delaying the completion of forms or by changing their diagnosis on individual patients. A few asylums tried to hide patients or to persuade their families to take them away.

The 'official' Aktion T4 disposed of 70,273 people. The same precise observation of fact and detail was made in assessing the savings to the country the elimination of these poor souls produced. In official T4 reports, graphs illustrated the money and the quantities of commodities saved.

Chapter Ten

Specific Disability Legislation

For many years in Britain charities had raised funds by depicting disabled people as objects of pity so that money could be found for their keep and welfare, usually in institutions. It was several generations later before organisations like the very vocal Disablement Income Group (DIG) – inspired by a Guardian article by Mary Stott, was founded by the admirable Megan Du Boisson. Later led by the remarkable Mary Greaves, and strongly supported by the Central Council for the Disabled, the DIG was driven on by Duncan Guthrie and then George Wilson – who mounted the first campaigns to provide a 'voice' for disabled people. The Victorian 'medical' model of disability began to crumble. At last it began to be regarded as a social model and, perhaps for the first time, as a human rights issue.

These first glimmers of new thinking, however, left disabled people themselves still closely controlled, still ignored, still hidden away. As the authors of '*As of Right*' said in 1985: 'In the whole field of social policy, there was no disadvantaged group so utterly neglected'.

In terms of care, there was little or nothing on the statute book that was specifically about the problems of disabled people. Before the Chronically Sick and Disabled Persons Act 1970 most of what little recognition or assistance was available to them under legislation had not been designed to meet their needs.

Made paupers by their disabilities, they could seek help under the many Poor Laws, but achieved it only with great difficulty due to harsh means-testing.

The first ever organisation of disabled people was the National League of the Blind and Disabled (NLBD), originally formed in branches around 1893, but subsequently affiliated to the TUC in 1902 and the Labour Party in 1909. The organisation was, and is, community based and has retained its campaigning ethic particularly through its consistent voice at Labour Party Conferences and Annual Conferences of the TUC.

In terms of training and employment, the focus was always on the needs of disabled ex-servicemen. In 1919 there was legislation to set up training centres for people disabled by war. The Blind Persons Act 1920 (an early notable success for NLBD following a 4- day march of blind people to Trafalgar Square to meet the Prime Minister) was enacted to provide instructional facilities for disabled ex-servicemen, but its provisions were to be extended to blind civilians. Parliament obviously needed war to give it impetus, for it was not until 1941, when there was a shortage of labour, that retraining facilities were extended to civilian disabled people. A committee known as the Interdepartmental Committee on the Rehabilitation and Resettlement of Disabled Persons, met under the chairmanship of George Tomlinson MP, and its recommendations became the Disabled Persons (Employment) Act 1944. This enabled retraining for all disabled people, irrespective of how their disability had come about. It was the first legislation to accept the principle that any disability constitutes a claim upon the state for assistance to enable the disabled person to be reinstated wherever possible into useful work. The Act provided for the first-ever register of disabled people, which made it mandatory for employers to have a quota of 3% of disabled people on their books. Sadly, this provision was almost totally ignored by employers, even Government departments, and no attempts were made to enforce it until 1974. Moreover, there was no perception in Parliament that there was an identifiable group of disabled people, other than ex-servicemen, urgently needing help.

Soldier at the battlefront WW1.

Blinded First World War soldier learns braille.

Meeting in Trafalgar Square.

Auschwitz after the Second World War where Alf Morris saw the piles of rusting wheelchairs.

Eileen Uttley, teaching speech to a group of deaf and disabled children some 45 years ago.

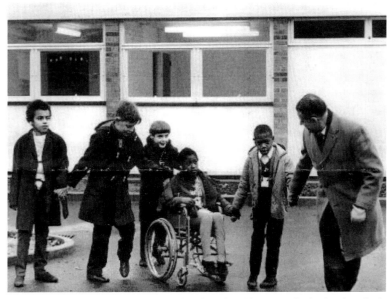

Denis Uttley (teacher of the deaf) and children from the Old Kent Road School with multiple disabilities…probably 50 years ago…

Alf Morris, visiting handicapped youngsters learning skills in new technology at Chailey Heritage, Sussex, when he was minister for disabled people.

Alf Morris in China with disabled children.

Lady Sue Masham arriving at House of Lords to make her maiden speech on Alf Morris' bill, 1970.

In 1945 the Disabled Persons Employment Corporation (Remploy) Act established a non-profit making company, Remploy, to provide sheltered employment for disabled people. Shortly afterwards, using the National Assistance Act 1948, some of the more enlightened local authorities did develop supporting services for disabled people through the back door. Section 29 of this allowed authorities to offer services to those who were in need 'by virtue of age or infirmity'.

But such provision was not mandatory, only permissive, and this resulted in some localities providing very limited availability of leisure opportunities and meals-on-wheels. Only a few identified and registered disabled people so that they could be given information about whatever was available to help them. There was the same random, under-enthusiastic response to their lead, principally because offering services cost the authority money and there was no duty to do anything.

The National Assistance Act 1948 placed a duty on local authorities to make residential care available to any older or disabled person who could not manage at home. However this was widely and wilfully misinterpreted by many local authorities. The best decided to establish purpose-built accommodation for disabled people. Others squashed older people and disabled people together whatever their ages. Yet others paid fees to have them accommodated in private or charitably-run provision, with little regard for the facilities or age ranges. Typically, the most readily available accommodation for disabled people was in homes primarily concerned with caring for older people.

The National Assistance Act's other aspects are seldom dwelt upon. It supported a network of Reception Centres offering very short-term accommodation to homeless and rootless people, many of whom were disabled either physically or mentally. Under Section 51 of the Act a man could be prosecuted for 'frequenting centres when he was able to maintain himself'. There were 134 such prosecutions in 1962, 180 in 1961 and 88 in 1960. These were of men who, in the National Assistance Board's view, could have worked but had persistently refused to do so. As a result in

1962, 81 men were sent to prison, while 33 were fined and 7 placed on probation.

By 1964 the number of men prosecuted had dropped to 16. The National Assistance Board, created by the Act, also had powers to prosecute those who did not behave themselves in the Reception Centres, particularly in terms of becoming unruly. The Board's 1964 report notes that there were 38 such prosecutions for breaches of the peace, and that in the 36 cases for which convictions were obtained 19 men were sent to prison.

The Mental Health Act 1959, which called for the discharge of more people from hospitals into community care, led to an increase in the numbers of homeless and rootless disabled people. It also enabled patients – provided they were not violent – to discharge themselves, leading to yet more pressure on the reception centres.

The limited help offered at these centres was geared towards encouraging people to a 'settled way of life', but this was a forlorn hope for many. J. Stuart Whiteley, Chief Assistant in the Department of Psychological Medicine at Westminster Hospital, made a study of people using a reception centre. He found that the common factor was social isolation. At its minimum their social isolation was shown by a disinclination to join in, at its maximum by the psychotic withdrawal of schizophrenia. He also discovered that 32% had either been in a mental hospital or exhibited symptoms of mental instability. Of these, Dr Whiteley said: 'Although so many have had mental illness, it does not entirely account for their present condition. When they became ill they were already segregated from family, friends and social contacts, and had no outside arm to support them. Even if they had some treatment, they were less equipped than most patients to cope with society when they were discharged from hospital, and they quickly sank into an environment which made no demands on them but equally awarded them no assistance...'

In 1965 a team of researchers at the Institute of Psychiatry, Maudsley Hospital, surveyed a sample of 51 homeless men using an East London soup kitchen. Twenty of them had at some time been in a mental hospital. Forty of them had spent some time in prison.

'The adult inability of these men to find roots seems to have been caused in the first instance not by their drinking, but by their damaged personalities, and the origin of this damage could often be seen in a children's home where the benefits of human contact were scant indeed,' said the research paper.'

The suspicion and then suppression of 'strange' rootless people, stems from the days of master and serf, when a working man had to belong to somebody, and had to stay in one place, or he was up to no good. Wayfarers of all kinds, and particularly those with disabilities, were treated harshly. Casual wards, where wayfarers could seek accommodation, had cells with them. In some, hunks of stone were put into each cell. Before he was released the following morning and given anything to eat, the man had to smash up the stone and push every splinter of it through the very small holes in the grill on the door. This was to illustrate that he had done some work to earn his night's keep.

The Disabled Persons(Employment) Act 1958, had as its aim the expansion of sheltered workshops for disabled people, and a very limited one it was too. In effect, the prospects for obtaining work or being trained for it, or of receiving financial help as of right, were extremely dismal. In large part disabled people were excluded from the National Insurance Scheme because 'having no prospect of employment' they lacked the stamps needed to entitle them to benefits. They were not opt-outs of the scheme, but left-outs.

Financially, disabled people had always suffered from having no benefit available to them as of right of disability. The earliest financial provision of any kind for them dates from the middle ages when common law made it possible to claim financial compensation for disabilities caused by negligence. The same right of compensation for disabilities caused by war service came in the sixteenth century. This was followed during the industrial revolution by the growth in insurance, largely provided by friendly societies and then trade unions, against industrial injuries, but all state provision focussed on war and industrial injuries. Originally for employees to gain compensation the injury had to be caused by the employer's negligence. But with the arrival of the Workmen's Compensation Acts of 1897 and 1906, compensation was paid even if the employer was not at fault.

For disabled people unable to work or to find work, the only resort was to the Poor Law system for the relief of destitution and dating back to the early seventeenth century. The Poor Laws of the nineteenth century were even harsher. Beveridge had the opportunity to replace centuries of a compensatory and means-tested culture when in 1942 he reviewed the social security system. His report stated that means-tested assistance was unacceptable, but he failed to achieve any fundamental change. He created no as-of-right benefits for long-term disability. What remained was the preferential continuance of treatment for those disabled at work or in war and short-term help for those who were sick or temporarily disabled, very much tied to a contributory National Insurance scheme. It was of no use at all to long-term disabled people who were unable to work. For them, the only 'lifeline' was the National Assistance Act 1948, modelled on the old Poor Law, which merely placed a duty upon the National Assistance Board to give means-tested help to people without resources, or whose resources needed to be supplemented.

The Supplementary Benefit Act 1966 was meant to do better, but its effect was still to leave disabled people having to plead poverty: it did nothing to help them out of dependence, or to encourage the development of skills to achieve the liberating status of securing a job and the dignity of becoming a tax payer. In fact, there were no significant improvements in social security for disabled people between 1946 and 1970. They mostly remained permanently poor, dependent on supplementary benefit, with no income as of right. Those with a social conscience had long been aware of the link between disability and poverty, but it was not until the results of Amelia Harris's survey of disabled people was published in the early 1970s that the extent of it was finally documented. Nearly a third of the disabled people in her sample were receiving supplementary benefit; seven per cent were living below the Government's official poverty line; and a further 170,000 had not claimed, either because they did not know of their entitlement or because of the stigmatising effects of means-testing.

The law was still focussed on providing welfare rather than creating independence. No legislation aimed at helping disabled people to lead fuller lives had ever found its way through Parliament. From 1945 to 1960 not a word appeared in the manifestos of the Labour or Conservative parties about disabled people and their needs, except in the context of disability due to service in the armed forces. In Labour's 1966 manifesto there was mention of disabled people, and just a brief word or two in that of the Conservatives. Between 1959 and 1964 the House of Commons did not debate disability once.

It was principally Alf Morris, MP for Manchester Wythenshawe, his Labour colleague Jack Ashley, MP for Stoke-on-Trent South and the Conservative John Astor who became the first to ask questions about a group of which Parliament seemed genuinely unaware – disabled people. Jack Ashley in 1968 attempted to bring in a one-clause Bill to set up a commission to research the problems of disabled people and the anomalies in their treatment, but he failed.

Outside the House also things were starting to happen in response to the lack of parliamentary concern. The Disablement Income Group (DIG) had been formed earlier in the 1960s with the object of pressing for an income for disabled people as of right. The Central Council for the Disabled (which later became RADAR), the Disabled Living Foundation and the National Campaign for the Young Chronic Sick began to campaign and lobby.

One breakthrough was the Seebohm report, a major investigation into the delivery of social services, which brought to public attention the extent of need among physically and mentally disabled people. Follow-up legislation was promised. Richard Crossman, Secretary of State for Social Services, was considering a National Superannuation and Social Insurance Bill, which would include an earnings-related invalidity pension. The Government was even aware that it needed to establish the parameters of disability, particularly the incidence and causes of disability. In a written reply to a parliamentary question in October 1967, the Health Minister stated that there was to be a major survey of disabled people.

Jack Ashley tried to put the case for a draft Bill – put together by Dr David Owen before he became a Minister - under which people who did not qualify under the National Insurance scheme would have for the first time obtained a pension. The draft also sought to make local authorities reserve council houses for disabled people and equip them accordingly. The Bill got no further than First Reading on February 21st 1969 when the Labour Government having already made it clear that it would block the measure, it was defeated by 112 to 76.

In the same year, the Conservative Gordon Campbell attempted to get legislation passed to set up an advisory commission to investigate pensions and benefits for disabled people. This too met Government opposition and was defeated in an almost empty house on Second Reading on March 28th by a derisory 28 votes to 24. Although these defeats were far from encouraging, the very existence of legislative activity showed that somewhere deep within the parliamentary heart was a stirring of support for disabled people.

The Disablement Income Group determined to present Whitehall and Westminister with the needs of disabled people. Lobbying and rallies in London in 1967-68 gradually brought more MPs into the fray and led to more frequent mentions of disability issues in Parliament. Largely through questions placed by Dr David Owen, John Astor, Jack Ashley, Alf Morris, Neil Martin, Lewis Carter-Jones and Dr Michael Winstanley there was a growing awareness within Parliament that public opinion wanted changes in official attitudes; from shades of charity to acceptance that disabled people should have the same rights as everyone else to live dignified lives within the community.

Chapter Eleven

Alf Morris

Despite the improvements in methods of preventing disability which developed in the nineteenth and twentieth centuries, this was not accompanied by any real change in society's attitudes towards disabled people themselves. They were still the bottom of the pile, shut away because of lack of access to transport and buildings, and made paupers by prejudice, lack of employment or an income of any kind by right.

Pivotol to the radical change for the better in their lives in the UK, and subsequently in other parts of the world, in the last third of the twentieth century, was the Chronically Sick and Disabled Persons Act 1970. Even the initiator of arguably the most famous Private Member's Bill ever, Alf Morris, now Lord Morris of Manchester, believes that it really was a miracle that it navigated the treacherous waters always experienced by such private attempts at legislation without ministerial backing. Its enactment, together with the fact that Alf Morris later became the UK's and the world's first-ever Minister for Disabled People which enabled him to ensure that it was justly enforced, led to doors being opened to opportunities for enriching the lives of disabled people never before thought possible or even imaginable.

When the time came for the annual ballot for Private Member's Bills in 1969, Alf Morris was on duty in India with a parliamentary delegation, but he arranged for Charles Morris, his brother, the MP for Manchester Openshaw and the Government's Deputy Chief Whip, to put forward his name. There are many fascinating stories behind the Chronically Sick and Disabled Persons Act itself, largely of party and parliamentary subterfuge, but none as fascinating as those which illustrate the tenacity and courage with which its architect hung on to the tail of the ferocious animal he had created as it fought its way through party and parliamentary intrigue and initial opposition.

Alf's personal experience with the Act began with a crumpled day-old newspaper which proved the herald of what was to come. He was travelling home from the Indian mission in November 1969 when he saw a copy of the *Guardian* left in the aircraft by a previous passenger. He was glancing idly through it when suddenly one headline made him look more intently: it contained the news that his name had been drawn first in the annual ballot which enables MPs to present Private Member's bills. Both exhilarated and somewhat overawed, he immediately began to write his first thoughts for a Chronically Sick and Disabled Persons Bill in an old address book

'When I won the opportunity to legislate in the Private Members' Ballot of November 1969,' he later wrote, 'there was no expensively pre-packed Bill for me to present. It has been said that my only possessions were a blank piece of paper and a burning conviction, but there was never any doubt what problems I would tackle.'

Alf Morris could not have been more suitable to become the human instrument needed to create and see the Act through to reality. Not only had he already shown himself to be an active constituency MP, but he had gained experience of higher government and the ministries involved as the Parliamentary Private Secretary to Fred Peart. Moreover, the main theme of his parliamentary career had already been stated and seen to be the problems and needs of disabled people. He was a member of the All-Party Disablement Group.

Alf Morris left school at the age of fourteen but, after doing his National Service from 1946-48, mainly with Middle East

Land Forces in Egypt and Palestine, in 1950 he won a place to read Modern History at Oxford University. He was already involved in politics, having joined the Labour Party and the Co-operative Party when he was sixteen. The first speech he made was as a Manchester delegate to the Co-operative Party's annual conference and was about preventable hardship among disabled people.

More importantly, he had real personal experience of disability and the poverty it brought with it. He lived with his parents and brothers and sisters in a slum in Ancoats, one of Manchester's poorest districts. His father, George Morris, was severely disabled in the First World War. Crippling leg injuries, partial blindness and the effects of being gassed on the Somme meant that he was often unable to work. Alf's mother bore the brunt of being both provider and carer. His father eventually died of heart failure accelerated by tuberculosis, at the age of 44 on the 11th November 1935, before Alf was eight years old. The experience seared into his conscience and heart. Only the widowed Mrs Morris's pride and insistence avoided her husband being buried direct from hospital into a pauper's grave, after a suggestion from Withington Hospital that he should be taken straight to the cemetery to cut costs. Even though his funeral took place from home it was into a grave without a stone.

'In the 1930s, even more than in post-war years, disablement was another word for poverty,' said Alf Morris. 'My mother would have said that it was often also another word for needless humiliation. When she sought to confirm her right to a war widow's pension, my mother found officialdom as intractable as it had previously been insensitive. I think we were first told that my father's war pension had died with him on the grounds that his death was not directly due to the injuries for which his pension had been awarded. The battle to reverse this decision was dour and protracted. The late Alderman Harry Thorneycroft, our Member of Parliament, was eventually asked to intervene on my mother's behalf. It was only then, three year's after my father's death, that my mother's status as a war widow was confirmed.

The battle raged long enough to leave me with a lasting interest in war pensions and the war disabled.'

Morris's mother would no doubt have been happy to know that he was, as an MP himself, able to introduce legislation to amend the War Pensions Act 1921 and the Pensions Tribunal Act 1943, to speed and simplify procedures for disabled ex-servicemen and their families.

'Although still less than eight years old, I had already experienced the realities of life for a disabled family,' said Morris. 'Ever since my childhood I have known that the quickest way to find a deprived child is first to find a disabled father. The child of a disabled parent is just as much involved in the problems of severe disablement as the parent of a disabled child. Whenever a severely disabled person is handicapped socially by avoidable restrictions on his mobility or his exclusion from inaccessible public and social buildings, his family also is socially handicapped. There are things other families can do that they cannot do. That is why I emphasised the importance of the concept of the disabled family.'

Morris's early personal experience of disability happened against a background of poverty and poor housing conditions. When he married, he moved into the home of his wife's parents, a household also crippled by disability, this time her mother's severe rheumatoid arthritis. This aspect of disability also did not go unnoticed. He realised as the law then stood that there was no legal requirement for local housing authorities to make special provision for the housing needs of disabled people.

This was the background that informed Alf Morris's desire to make life better for chronically sick and disabled people. The earliest indication that he might personally be able to promote that desire came when he became the MP for Wythenshawe, Manchester, in October 1964, after first fighting elections in the Garston division of Liverpool in 1951 and Wythenshawe as prospective Labour candidate in 1959. In the House between 1964 and 1969 he asked scores of questions intended to try to make life better for disabled people, and spoke in a number of debates. Many of those questions were reflected in the provisions of the Chronically Sick and Disabled Persons Act that Alf Morris eventually initiated.

When he had picked up that newspaper in the plane from India, it was not surprising that he should think of legislation to revolutionise the lives of disabled people. One of his recurring questions had revolved around the fact that not enough was known about the number of disabled people and that a register needed to be established so that they could be identified and offered help. This was the first thing he scrawled across his address book.

He had also asked many questions on the thorny issue of access for disabled people. For example, the number of lavatories which were accessible to people in wheelchairs; how they were, or rather were not, able to travel; how they were not able to enjoy leisure opportunities like others because they could not get into means of transport, or places of education and entertainment.

'I wanted to remove the severe and gratuitous social handicaps inflicted on disabled people, and often their families and friends, not just their exclusion from town and county halls, art galleries, libraries and most of the universities, but even from pubs, restaurants, theatres, cinemas and other places of entertainment,' explained Alf Morris. 'I knew that opening doors to disabled people was of fundamental importance to improving their social status. Their forced exclusion from public and social buildings makes them feel like a race apart. In seeking to throw open the doors of these buildings, I was concerned to stop society from treating disabled people as if they were a separate species.'

He also recognised that there were specific problems for young disabled people. Many of those who were chronically ill were in geriatric wards simply because there was no other provision. Besides these there were young homeless disabled people living mostly among older residents in local authority homes.

'Then there were the problems of housing for severely disabled people living at home, the special educational problems of severely handicapped children, mobility and employment problems and many others, including the need to make sure that disabled people were given their proper place in advising Ministers and other policy-makers on decisions affecting their lives,' said Alf Morris.

'There was also the need to increase spending on technological aids and research and development in the service of disabled people. For military purposes, resources for research and development were plentiful, but for the purpose of helping to normalise the lives of disabled people, such resources were extremely scarce.'

Those were Alf Morris's early thoughts as, still clutching the crumpled copy of the newspaper he had found, he descended from the plane at Heathrow. He could not have foreseen the roller coaster of a ride, and the subsequent stress and strain, the luck of the draw would bring him.

Chapter Twelve

The Big Act

Alf Morris arrived in Westminster from New Dehli to find his desk top already hidden under a pile of correspondence from people all too willing to advise him on the subject matter of the Bill he should introduce. From that moment, any doubts he may have had about the immensity and the responsibilities of the task he faced disappeared. There were hundreds of different suggestions for a Bill. As well as those from outside organisations and pressure groups, there were also many from Government departments who wanted to push through legislation for which there was no parliamentary time available to ministers. Accepting one of those departmental alternatives would have made Alf Morris's life a great deal easier. Bill drafting and secretarial assistance would automatically have been made available. If he decided to go it alone and produce his own Bill on disability none of this would be forthcoming. Despite that, he decided that he should pursue his own course.

It was also a race against time. Only twenty days in each parliamentary session are allowed for Private Members' business. Of those twenty days, only ten are available for Private Members' legislation, the remaining days being devoted to Private Members' motions. It has always been this miserly allowance of time that is the chief opponent of any Private Members' Bills. Formal Government legislation receives the benefit of room having been made in the parliamentary timetable to allow for it to become law. In the case of Private Member's Bills no such time is allowed, and in the absence of an unopposed Second Reading they will fail. However, around six days are devoted to Second Reading debates and Alf Morris, having won first place in the ballot, was considered in theory to have a very real chance of getting a measure through to legislation. Even then, the Government's attitude to a Private Member's Bill is crucial. If the Government lets it be known that it opposes the measure it is usually 'talked out' and suffers defeat.

There are other pitfalls. Since Private Member's Bills are always debated on a Friday, when many MPs get away to deal with constituency business, there is often a limited number of supporters available to vote. It is then possible for any quite small group to gain enough votes to defeat the Bill. When Alf Morris arrived back from India, he had already lost time. The ballot for Private Members' Bills is held under House Standing Orders on the second Thursday of the parliamentary session. Those successful must present their Bills at the start of business on the 5th Wednesday of the session. In 1969 the ballot was held on the 6th November, but because Alf Morris was away in India on that day he did not hear of his success until November 8th. This meant that he had not only to decide on the subject for his Bill but present it for First Reading within 18 days, that is on November 26th. That was not such a problem because all that would be needed for this was a title and a dummy Bill. However, the reality was that he still had only three weeks in which to produce and publish a Bill for the day allocated, December 5th, for its Second Reading in the House of Commons, and that was very important. If the Morris Bill was to claim its place in the parliamentary timetable and stay at the head of the queue for parliamentary time, he had to have the Bill fully drafted well before that date. It is the practice in the House that Members should not have to face the Second Reading of a Bill without having had due time to study its contents and implications. Because it must be presented in a fully printed form, the copy for it must be ready at least a week before the date of the Second

Reading. Otherwise it would slide down the line and any chance of taking it through to legislation would be considerably reduced. The demands of Father Time presented considerable strain for the Bill's creator. It was not to prove an easy ride.

The major problem was that its aims and purposes 'trespassed' into the territories of several different ministries, indeed those of twelve Departments of State. The first opposition came from an unexpected quarter. Richard Crossman, the Secretary of State for Social Services, called Alf to his office. Ironically, as Alf entered he was confronted by the heavily bandaged foot of the Minister sprawled across the elegant red surface of his desk to try to relieve the pain.

Crossman told him in no uncertain terms that he should drop any thought of a Chronically Sick and Disabled Persons Bill. 'If we had needed a disability Bill,' Crossman winced, 'I would have introduced and enacted it myself.'

At the time the Secretary of State was himself heavily engaged in putting together his own Bill to bring in a new State Pension Scheme, and it could have been that he thought Morris's efforts would cut across this. He then suggested that Morris should introduce a Bill on the transplantation of kidneys and other organs, and hinted that then he would be able to let him have help with the drafting, whereas none would be available if he insisted on introducing his Disability Bill. Alf's friends were disappointed with the Crossman response, but urged him to continue with his original intentions, even though it was impossible to see how he could succeed without Crossman's support.

In this encounter, and the many others that took place in those dramatic three weeks, Alf stuck to his guns. At that stage, he still had little more than the jottings in the old address book. He now had only two weeks left of the twenty days in which to have ready the finished long title of the Bill. After that there remained only a week in which to produce the Bill itself.

In reality Alf Morris only succeeded in meeting this deadline because of the crucial assistance of four individuals. One was Whitehall's principal parliamentary draftsman who secretly helped in improving the drafting of the Bill, as did Giles Eccle-stone who worked in the Public Bill Office and acted as Clerk to the Standing Committee. The parliamentary draftsman gave his help privately and in his own time because he had a disabled daughter and saw the necessity for legislation on disability. Another offering drafting and legal advice was David Weitzman, QC, who also became a member of the Standing Committee. The fourth person was a good parliamentary friend Fred Peart, the former Minister for Agriculture and then Leader of the House, who, in particular, assisted in breaching the many ministerial barriers which stood in the Bill's path.

Statistical information to help Alf Morris frame his Bill was difficult to find, if indeed it existed. Despite the dire situation in which hundreds of disabled young people were trapped in long-stay hospital wards, for instance, he discovered that nobody knew exactly how many were trapped in these places. He asked parliamentary question after question, but nobody could give him a figure. Indeed, on all aspects of disability, statistics proved the highest hurdle wherever Morris turned. He was fully aware that policy making would be difficult without the ability to identify and count the number of people needing services. Everybody knew there were many such people, but nobody could say exactly how many. There were 235,000 disabled people on the disable-ment registers kept by local authorities, but it seemed only too obvious, as Morris sought evidence from organisations working with disabled people, that the real figure was at least six times that number. The best 'guess' – from social scientist Peter Townsend – was that there were about 1.2 million disabled people. The Dis-ablement Income Group, which had undertaken some research itself, was claiming that the figure was some 1.5 millions. Such guesswork provided no practical basis for planning services. It was, in fact, only after Amelia Harris's national survey was published in 1971, revealing that over a third of the population were either disabled or significantly affected by somebody else's disability, that the immense size of the problem was revealed. 'Disability in Great Britain', the 1996/1997 disability follow-up to the Family Resources Survey, showed that more than 8,500.000 adults in Great Britain had a disability.

'All we could guess then was that there were upwards of one million severely disabled people in need of help whose identities were unknown to public authority,' reflects Morris. 'I found that even the keeping of local disablement registers was permissive. The local councils could virtually decide for themselves whether such registers should be kept. They were kept under Section 29 of the National Assistance Act 1948, and recorded the cases only of people receiving some kind of help from the council. They were certainly not registers of the actual incidence of severe disablement in any locality.

'Local authority services for disabled people were as permissive as registration and they too were based on Section 29 of the 1948 Act,' said Morris. 'We knew it would be essential to amend that Act if we were to ensure a high standard of local services. Knowing also how little most local authorities were then providing, we were determined to disturb their smug complacency and make them do for the chronically sick and disabled what they had failed to do when given the opportunity.'

Indeed, the truth was that nobody knew the national reality or impact of disability. One of Morris's first strategies was to encourage the Ministries, Parliamentarians and external organisations to submit ideas. These came from both sides of the House. The Labour helpfuls included Jack Ashley, Lewis Carter-Jones, Fred Evans, (MP for Caerphilly), John Golding, (MP for Newcastle-under-Lyme), and Arthur Latham. From the Conservatives came ready help from Neil Marten, (MP for Banbury, former junior Minister and Chairman of the All-Party Disabled Drivers Group), Maurice Macmillan, John Astor, Sir Clive Bossom, Dame Irene Ward and Sir Brandon Rhys-Williams. However, there was still not wholehearted approval from any of the Ministries across whose territories its provisions extended, and, although Morris would never then admit it, there was very little encouragement either. Nobody, for instance, offered to adopt the Bill largely because there was a lot of extra work, and possibly expense, involved for them in its propositions. There was, in fact, a strong possibility at one stage that the Government would flatly oppose it. This did not happen because two key Government Ministers had privately decided that it was a constructive measure, much needed, and gave it their support. These were the Chief Whip, Bob Mellish, and Fred Peart, and they worked hard out of the limelight to make sure it would be given a fair run.

So it was that, on 5th December 1969, Alf Morris was able to move the Second Reading of the Chronically Sick and Disabled Persons Bill. 'What most disabled people want more than anything else is to lessen their dependence on other people, to get on with living their own lives as normally as they can in their own homes among their own family and, wherever possible, to have the opportunity of contributing to industry and society as fully as their abilities allow,' he told the House. 'Investment in people, disabled people no less than fit and strong and fortunate people, is much the best of all investments.'

A crucially important part of the Bill was to be found in its first section which demanded, and made mandatory, a mind-change in those authorities, especially local authorities, who should have been assisting disabled people. It would become a duty for them to seek out disabled people and keep a record; to say how many there were and inform them of services available to them. This meant that it was no longer good enough for them merely to answer to the needs of those who actually asked for help: councils had to find and do something for those who did not. Previously, there had been a register for the blind, and, under the 1948 National Assistance Act, local authorities had an obligation to keep a record of disabled people who came to them for assistance. The effect of that legislation was, however, that authorities who were reluctant to spend money on helping disabled people could restrict publicity about the help available.

The second section of Morris's Bill then made the very important link between finding the people and establishing what they needed. Local authorities had to undertake this research and then provide for the needs they uncovered.

Housing also featured strongly in the Bill, reflecting Morris's childhood and early marital experiences in Manchester. Local authorities would be statutorily required to take the needs of disabled people into account in future housing developments. Access was a major feature. The Bill provided that a duty be placed on the owner of any new building open to the public, be it for leisure, pleasure or work, to provide means of access and toilet facilities for disabled people. No planning permission would be given until these requirements were met. Access and facilities within them was particularly emphasised in schools and universities. Hotels, restaurants, cinemas, theatres and all other places of entertainment were also required to provide accessible toilet facilities. Disabled parking places had to be available.

The problem Morris had identified earlier of young disabled people being trapped in long-stay geriatric wards was addressed, as were those kept in residential homes for elderly people. He was also faithful to the memory of his mother's struggle to get a war widow's pension: the Bill made changes in the way war pensions appeals were dealt with which made the process many times quicker.

The special educational needs of severely disabled children were addressed through changes to the Education Act 1944. There was a special emphasis on deaf-blind, dyslexic and autistic children, and others with childhood psychosis.

Alf Morris, as always, eloquently introduced his Bill for a Second Reading by expressing his own high ideals and hopes for disabled people.

'We must seek a society' he said 'in which there is genuine respect for people with disabilities; where understanding is unostentatious and sincere; where if years cannot be added to the lives of the most severly disabled, at least life can be added to their years; where needs come before means; where the mobility of disabled people is restricted only by the bounds of technical progress and discovery; where they have a fundamental right to participate in industry and society according to their ability; where socially preventable distress is unknown; and where no-one has cause to feel ill-at-ease because of his disability.'

It was soon to become apparent, however, that there were still severe reservations, verging on hostility, towards Morris's Bill in some quarters. Richard Crossman was absent at this Second Reading. It was left to Dr John Dunwoody, Under Secretary of State at the Department of Health and Social Security, to voice reservations in the chamber. His coolness obviously reflected the attitude of his boss, the absent Secretary of State. Dunwoody made it plain that areas in the Bill which touched upon social security benefits would have to be looked at in conjunction with the National Superannuation Bill, which would be put before the House shortly by his Department. He also made the point that a Government social survey on the disabled and handicapped was proceeding and suggested that it would be as well to wait until the results of that were known before rushing to take the Morris Bill onto the statute book. Dunwoody also cautioned that there was a problem with money, since there was in place a limit on the growth of public spending until the economy stabilised. However, grudgingly, he added that he hoped the Bill would be given its Second Reading.

The real hope of Crossman and the Ministry was obviously that it would fail to get a final reading after its committee stage. In the event, the Commons did give the Bill a Second Reading, but now it faced its committee stage at which it would be scrutinised word by word. A committee will usually have on it a majority of people favourable towards the measure, but this does not always guarantee success. It is still possible for opponents to table so many amendments and insist on speaking at length on them with the result that it loses its place in the queue for the limited amount of parliamentary time devoted to Private Members' legislation and is killed.

This was where the power struggle between no fewer than twelve different Ministries was soon to become apparent. Morris himself was totally engaged in the daunting task of polishing-up the hastily constructed Bill, and redrafting and reshaping it in the light of the Second Reading debate and of other views and comments made to him since then. At the same time, he was under severe pressure from the conflicting interests of the different Ministries and Ministers, and acting as his own unofficial 'whip' to ensure that each committee meeting had enough supporters of the Bill present to ensure progress.

He was even responsible for ensuring that a quorum was present at all times so that meetings were not suspended for the lack of one. Morris hoped that he would be able to struggle on until the Christmas recess gave him more time to undertake the redrafting. The committee stage started on the 17th December, and, as was customary, Alf Morris immediately introduced a sittings motion, stating that the committee should meet again on January 21st and then on each Wednesday morning at 10.30. Because of the work that was still being undertaken on its early clauses, Morris was forced to ask that the committee scrutinise the Bill in reverse order, looking at some of its last clauses first. He was literally drafting the Bill on his feet as he took in changes and new suggestions from colleagues and outside organisations.

The first clause moved was No. 29, which, with the support of the Ministry of Transport, would allow invalid carriages to be used on pavements. This went well, and the committee agreed to approve the clause without a division. This set an unusual pattern: throughout the Chronically Sick and Disabled Persons Bill's passage through its committee stage, it was never necessary to call for a division. However, it was the next clause considered, No.26, which brought out the worst in a suspicious Ministry. Tony Benn, Technology Minister, had agreed with Alf that there should be a clause to the effect that his Ministry would have to report annually to Parliament on what had been achieved in applying technology to help disabled people. It seemed a sensible idea, but when Dr John Dunwoody spoke it was clear that the Health Department was suspicious of such an approach, adding that his own Ministry would be largely responsible for such a report and that they produced two a year already. Dunwoody asked whether Morris would be prepared to withdraw the clause on the grounds that, because of lack of time, his Department had not been able to consider it properly. Alf Morris consulted his colleagues, particularly Jack Ashley and Dame Irene Ward, and decided not to withdraw the clause until the report stage which would allow time for the Government to come up with an alternative amendment or a new clause to meet their own reservations.

The first sitting of the committee was notable also for the debate which arose around one of the Bill's central issues: what responsibilities it placed upon local authorities. There was some discussion around whether the duty to be imposed upon them should be a duty to 'have regard so far as as practicable to the needs of disabled people', or should be expressed somewhat more strongly. Many members were worried that this wording gave local authorities too much discretion. Fred Evans, for example, said that Alf Morris should 'fight as hard as possible to prevent too much discretionary language creeping into the Bill and whenever possible to see that the duties laid upon local authorities were mandatory'.

The pressures on him were mounting. As well as having to consult and draft his Bill as he went along, he was also having to deal with the hundreds of letters a day that were now flooding in from disabled people themselves and organisations representing them. For a time he feared he would be drowned under this flood, but help came from Duncan Guthrie, Director of the Central Council for the Disabled, who offered secretarial assistance to deal with the correspondence.

The pressures on individual Ministers were equally onerous. Disability organisations maintained their lobbying, insisting that the Morris Bill should be supported and allowed to go onto the Statute Book. As the Bill continued its laborious way through its committee stage, there were signs at last that this pressure and Alf's meticulous consultations were paying dividends.

There were signs of growing Government support. The second sitting of the committee on January 17th demonstrated this. The committee considered a new clause drafted by the Ministry of Housing and Local Government and moved by the Minister, Reg Freeson. Alf Morris acknowledged the sympathetic attitude of his Ministry and the assistance from Reg Freeson personally. There was a second example: Morris had introduced a new clause dealing with access for disabled people to toilets in public buildings other than those for which local authorities were responsible. Alf said that this would touch upon the responsibilities of a number of Ministries other than Housing and Local Government, and that he supposed there would need to be consultation. Reg Freeson was able to surprise him by replying that these consultations had already taken place, and the other Ministries had indicated that they did not wish to oppose the clause. By this time Alf Morris began to feel that he had a good relationship with the Ministries affected by the Bill. His initial concern, after his meeting with Richard Crossman, that he was being rebuffed by the Government largely disappeared. This transformation went further when a number of clauses and amendments were introduced formally by Government departments.

The third committee sitting on January 28th 1970 demonstrated further help from a Government department, that of Education and Science. It provided considerable assistance in drafting Clause 31, which concerned special education for deaf-blind children. This had been promoted by Jack Ashley, and Alf paid tribute both to the efforts of Jack and the Ministry. Morris was again able to express his thanks for the help he had received from the DHSS and parliamentary counsel when he introduced his new Clause 8, which made amendments to speed up the procedures for war pension appeals.

However, by far the most important Government encouragement at this stage involved finance. One of the shortcomings of a Private Member's Bill is the rule that only the Government can bring in a Bill which imposes a cost on national revenues. This means that for a Private Member's Bill to succeed it must have no financial implications for the nation, or it must win from the Government what is known as a Financial Resolution to meet the spending involved. That the Bill involved spending public money but was not supported by a Government Money Resolution had been raised during the Bill's Second Reading, but it had still managed to get through three sittings of its committee stage without a Money Resolution. There was a crucial moment ahead when it would be possible to challenge and defeat the Bill on financial grounds.

It came when clauses in Sections 1 and 2, which had profound financial implications, came up for consideration. Fortunately, Alf had a friend and a considerable ally in the form of Bob Mellish, the Government Chief Whip, who arranged a meeting of the Ministers involved and told them it was now in the Government's interest to be seen as supportive of the Bill and that this would involve passing a Money Resolution. Alf Morris's Bill was awarded the accolade of a Money Resolution in Parliament which meant that funds could be spent to implement the Bill should it become law. Without this resolution, the Bill would not have survived.

At the fourth sitting, the Chairman, Sir Myer Galpern, reported that a Money Resolution had been moved relating to Clause 31. This was the main expenditure clause, which eventually became Clause 2. The Committee then debated a new Clause 30, which replaced Clauses 1 and 2 of the Bill as originally drafted by Alf. This was where major changes, which later heavily influenced the implementation of the subsequent Act, were made. Instead of requiring local authorities to maintain a register of all disabled people, as was originally hoped for, the clause now imposed a duty upon local authorities to take such steps as were reasonable and practicable to inform themselves of the number of disabled people in their areas. This new clause was welcomed by Dr John Dunwoody. An attempt was made to raise the question of full registration, but the Chairman ruled this was out of order because it did not arise under the new clause. Morris was fully aware of the implications of this change, but said it had been influenced by the arguments put up that if it became an absolute duty of local authorities to register all disabled people it would not be compatible with the principle that names should only be put on the register with the consent of the disabled people themselves and indeed disability organisations had insisted on voluntaryism and confidentiality. There is no doubt that the change did cause problems when the Act came to be implemented, but for many supporters it was seen as part of the price paid to move forward.

The committee then considered a new Clause 31, the provision which eventually became Section 2, and which imposed mandatory obligations on local authorities to meet the special needs of disabled people. A new Clause 32 was moved by Reg Freeson, the Housing Minister, and covered the housing needs of disabled people. He was also involved in moving a new Clause 33, which made it necessary for any person providing premises which included conveniences for the use of members of the public should also have regard, as far as practicable, to the needs of disabled people. A raft of other clauses had to be dropped because they were not covered by the Financial Resolution and could not therefore be considered. Dame Irene Ward raised the question of whether there was any possibility of amending the Financial Resolution so that these clauses might be included. The Chairman said this was not possible.

Alf Morris, aware of all the pitfalls ahead, was anxious that the committee should finish its work by the end of its fourth sitting and his wish was granted. The committee agreed that it had completed its work and that the Bill should be "reported to the House of Commons as amended," thus moving the Bill on towards further consideration by the House as a whole. Parliamentary commentators have observed that the Chronically Sick and Disabled Persons Bill was remarkable in its committee stage for the constructive manner in which MPs from all parties worked together.

The Bill appeared on the floor of the House of Commons for its Report Stage and Third Reading on the 20th March 1970. Speaking on that occasion Alf Morris identified another threat which might bar its progress, that of available time being squeezed still further. Although the Bill was now making sufficient progress for it to become law by August, there were strong rumours that the Prime Minister, Harold Wilson, might opt for an early General Election in June. That would mean that the legislative process required a very strong sprint up the home straight for Alf to succeed. All he could do was to keep up whatever pressure he and his supporters could provide, and hope for the best.

As usual with Private Members' Bills the Report Stage and Third Reading came on a Friday at 11 am. Mr. Speaker, Dr Horace King, warned that if the work on the Order Paper was to be completed, speeches would need to be short. Alf Morris began by moving a new clause about the provision by local authorities of information about the availability of chiropody services for disabled people. There was a strong sense among some backbenchers that certain clauses or new amendments would need to be abandoned in the light of opposition by the Government ministers involved in the interest of getting the Bill onto the Statute Book. The House then accepted two new clauses.

One, which became Section 22 of the Act, confirmed a promise given by Dr Dunwoody at the committee stage that he would replace the original Clause 26 with more appropriate provision. The second, which became Section 4, was tabled and moved by Reg Freeson to cover the ground previously covered by three earlier clauses. This imposed an obligation on those providing buildings where parking and toilet arrangements were open to the public to have a regard to the needs of disabled people.

Jack Ashley gave help with two new clauses, which eventually became Sections 26 and 27 of the Act and covered the special educational needs of autistic and dyslexic children. Gerry Fowler, for the Department of Education and Science, said that the Government accepted the new clauses and commended them to the House. There followed amendments which constituted another attempt to tighten up those provisions and which allowed local authorities discretion in undertaking the duties imposed on them, but Dr John Dunwoody raised practical difficulties. He then gave a vague undertaking that the Government would further consider the matter so that the amendments could be withdrawn.

One important amendment, which the House approved, was that the provisions of the Act should be extended to Scotland. There were many other amendments discussed before the Report stage was completed at 3 pm. Alf Morris then moved that his Bill be read a third time. He referred to the considerable help he had received from the All-Party Disablement Group, particularly Jack Ashley and John Astor, and thanked the many voluntarily agencies that had played a part.

However, once again Alf Morris displayed his visionary approach, when he said there really should be a Minister for Disabled People. This was his way of thanking Dr Dunwoody and Reg Freeson, whom he described as Joint 'Ministers for Disabled People'. He also expressed particular pleasure at the passing of Clause 23, which covered war pensions, and the relationship of this to the experience of his own father and mother.

Dr John Dunwoody now lavished praise on Alf Morris for his tenacity. Jack Ashley paid tribute to the Government: 'All the work which has been put in by the Government has not been visible. It has been like a duck's feet. They have been paddling away like mad, but the work has not been visible in the House…What the Bill has done is to focus the public mind and the minds of Hon. Members on the general problems and the vast range of disablement.'

The Bill thus completed its Commons stages and was put forward for the attention of the Peers after the Easter recess. The Bill appeared for Second Reading in the House of Lords on the 9th April. The first row of the cross benches was removed so that a particularly relevant group of Peers, (Baroness Masham, Lady Darcy de Knayth, Lord Ingleby, and Lord Crawshaw), four of the disabled members now to become known as the wheelchair bench, could be present to give their support. With their help, including a stirring maiden speech from the thirty-four-year-old Baroness Masham, the Bill survived its Second Reading, but by then the speculation about a June election was growing. It was almost accepted that Harold Wilson would go to the country, even though it appeared that a great deal of good legislation, including the Morris Bill, would go to the wall. He had already made it clear that he would call an election when the opinion polls showed Labour with a lead. That lead had now been established.

The Lords' committee stage began on the 30th April. The hazards to its progress were now entirely different. Its supporters in the Lords were so enthusiastic that they were in danger of killing it off with kindness by trying to squeeze more good things into it than was possible in the time available. It faced no fewer than fifteen pages of amendments tabled by their Lordships. There were pleas from supporters that they should not spend too long over these, but Lord Longford, a very recent ex-member of the Cabinet, insisted that members should give the Bill their usual thorough scrutiny. At the same time, Baroness Serota, Minister of State for Health and Social Security, was still emphasising to the committee the financial difficulties and the pressures on local authorities of the provision within the Bill for the registration of all disabled people. Alf Morris feared the worst: that all the burning of midnight oil, all the fights with Ministers and Ministries, all the persuading, would be sacrificed on the floor of the House of Lords.

When the committee met again on the 15th May even Lord Longford was convinced that there was going to be a General Election the following month. He now pleaded that there should be 'some adjustment in attitude, although I am not suggesting there should be unconditional surrender'. The Tories climbed on the anxiety bandwagon, realising that there were possibly several million votes from disabled people that could be swung their way. Lord Balniel, Tory Health spokesman in the Commons, pledged that if the Morris Bill ran out of time and was lost, they would bring it in as a Government measure immediately they were returned to power.

It may have been this that caused Harold Wilson to intervene. He quietly communicated to Ministers that the Morris Bill must be the one piece of legislation that got through before the election. This put a firework under their Lordships. To complete their debates on the Bill they met after dinner on at least one evening – an event then almost unheard of – and this speeded its return to the Commons for members to discuss the amendments made by the Lords. Two days later the Bill received the Royal Assent. It was the last Bill to become law before Parliament was dissolved for the General Election (an election which, ironically, the Tories won), but it became the first Act in British history and the world to give rights to disabled people. One jubilant campaigner, Duncan Guthrie, widely respected among disabled people, described it as their Magna Carta.

Some sections of the original Bill had fallen before its enactment, after being opposed by the Government or withdrawn during the committee stage. These included a review of the vehicle service for disabled people, particularly the replacement of the despised three-wheeled invalid 'car' with a four wheeled version, and the earnings rule for wives with long-term illnesses.

It really was a parliamentary miracle that Alf Morris's Act got through when so much other legislation was sacrificed.

Chapter Thirteen

After the Act

Despite the opinion polls, it was under the Tories that twenty-two of the twenty-nine sections of the Chronically Sick and Disabled Persons Act 1970 came into force on the 29th August 1970. In fact, the most important section of the Act did not come into operation until October 1971. This was because after they won power, Sir Keith Joseph (Secretary of State for Health and Social Security in the new Government), put out a circular telling the local authorities that it was not a requirement of Section 1 of the Act that they must attempt a one hundred percent identification and registration of disabled people. This despite the fact that the section clearly placed a responsibility on local authorities to search for all disabled people in their areas, register them, and offer them all benefits and services available. The Tories, deeply worried about the financial implications, gave the excuse that if they did go for one hundred percent registration it would consume all the resources so that there would be no funds remaining to meet the needs of the disabled people uncovered by the survey. They did suggest that sampling techniques would identify the actual numbers needing help, but made no firm suggestions about how local authorities should identify individuals and their personal needs. Yet unquestionably the Act was about identifying individual needs. And thus what the Act's author and backers now faced was not just a narrow, mean and nasty interpretation of Section 1 of the Act but an outright betrayal of its purpose.

Government departments were also extremely slow in getting out publicity material and raising awareness about the Act. Many disabled people who went to local authorities for help under its provisions, were asked what Act they were talking about. Undoubtedly some local authorities wilfully ducked their new responsibilities under the welfare sections, which covered help at home and the aids needed to live independently. Others said they could not proceed because Section 1 had been delayed. Telephones, which the Act specifically said should be supplied, were a particularly thorny issue.

Things got so bad that by December a Commons debate was demanded on the way the Act was being, or rather not being, implemented. MPs provided details of local authorities who were still denying all knowledge of it. The Government produced the same tired argument to defend itself – if it did fully implement Section 1 and seek out all disabled people, the entire welfare budget would go on this with nothing left for 'real' welfare.

Alf Morris of course joined the fray, pointing out for the umpteenth time that the implementation of Section 1 of the Act was greatly needed because it was the only way to help some of Britain's poorest and most needful people.

The debate appeared to do nothing to dent the Government's resolve not to move on an Act which had been supported by MPs from all parties as it struggled through the complexities of parliamentary processes less than a year previously. Early in February 1971 Jack Ashley was so incensed at this betrayal that – Alf Morris by then being a front bencher – he took a deputation of MPs to see Sir Keith Joseph. Their demand was that Section 1 be implemented immediately. From the Opposition Front Bench, Alf Morris expressed justified discontent when on the 27th February he went public with an accusation that some local authorities were openly turning their backs on their obligations under the Act. The trigger for Alf's ire was a memorandum from the County Councils Association and the Association of Municipal

Corporations that interpreted sections of the Morris Act in a particularly penny-pinching and mean-spirited manner.

'A document has come into my hands that prompts me to warn these authorities to stop tampering with the law,' Alf thundered. 'It is a hard-faced and cynical blueprint for diluting and evading the purpose of the law. Any County Council now considering the plan must be left in no doubt that it is both inexcusable and intolerable. It will be strenuously and implacably opposed.'

Far from moving the Government and local authorities faster towards the inevitability of what they must do, it only seemed to slow them down. In answer to a parliamentary question, Sir Keith Joseph had already said some months earlier that it was the intention to enforce Section 1 of the Act, to find and register all disabled people, on 1st April. He now announced that this would not take effect until the 1st October. It was plainly a signal to the local authorities that they need do nothing.

However, the Government failed to see that by procrastinating it was sitting on an unexploded bomb. In May came a publication which greatly embarrassed them. There appeared the report of a Government survey, triggered by the Wilson administration, of the numbers of "handicapped and impaired people" in Britain. It was the now-famous research undertaken by Amelia Harris, assisted by Elizabeth Cox, Christopher Smith and Judith Buckle, and it showed that there were over three million people in Britain suffering from some impairment. With the old registrations under the National Assistance Act showing only just over 200,000 disabled people, there was clearly a hidden problem representing poverty, neglect and suffering on a huge scale.

Just before the first anniversary of the Morris Act becoming law, Lewis Carter-Jones managed to force a Private Member's debate in the House which, in the face of the results of the Amelia Harris survey, demanded that the Act must now be fully implemented, by the Government and the local authorities. There were sharp exchanges, with Sir Keith Joseph actually trying to maintain that the Financial Resolution passed by the previous Labour Government was not a commitment to increase spending so that the Morris Act could be implemented, but just an authority to do so.

However, there were some signs that the Government's resolve to go slow was weakening and the chains around its coffers were slackening. It made provision for a increase of 12% in local authority spending on services for disabled people in the year 1971-72, and then that this should be doubled the next year to help meet the cost of Section 2 of the Act, which required local authorities to provide services. A further £3 million was committed to the building of hospital units for the young chronic sick, as envisaged by the Act, so that some of them could be released from their entrapment in geriatric wards.

Yet another £12 million a year was found to meet a new Attendance Allowance to help families who cared for disabled people at home, a measure strongly promoted by the National Council for Single Women and their Dependents, later to become the Carers National Association (of which, incidentally Sir Keith Joseph had been Chairman before coming into power). It was obvious that the relentless pressure exerted by Alf Morris, and disabled people themselves and the campaigning organisations that supported their case, was at last having some effect. At the same time, some boroughs were taking the provisions of the Morris Act very seriously indeed. In Liverpool, after some proactive seeking out, the numbers of registered disabled people rose by well over 100%, from 4,700 to 11,000 during just one year. In Manchester new cases were being added to the register at a rate of 5,000 a year. Two-thirds of the boroughs had taken action. The very fact that an Act now existed was exerting a strong influence on how people, especially local authorities, regarded and treated disabled people, despite the fact that ministers were not giving it their full support.

'The Act's furtive opponents have not saved public money by failing to provide the new charter of local services for disabled people,' said Alf Morris when he waded into the fray to add his voice to those condemning those local authorities, and some MPs who encouraged them, who were not meeting their commitments. 'In fact they have wasted public money. For the severely handicapped person who is not helped to live at home often has to be hospitalised, or otherwise institutionalised, at very much higher cost to public funds.'

The high profile the Act had received as it passed through Parliament was paying many dividends. Newspapers, especially local weeklies and provincial dailies, were now asking questions about how much local authorities were spending and about whether new buildings were making provision for disabled access under the Act. The glare of publicity even made the Government change its tune. The message of Sir Keith Joseph's infamous circular of August 1970, in which he told local authorities that it was not a requirement that they seek out disabled people under Section 1, was reversed in a September 1971 circular.

It informed local authorities that since they would ultimately be faced with the task of identifying all disabled people and meeting their needs, they should get on with it.

Over all, the verdict on the Morris Act of those who had reason to follow closely the fortunes of disabled people was much like that expressed by Duncan Guthrie: 'It has produced a wonderful change in the position of disabled people. As a result of the great publicity it has attracted public attitudes have changed.'

However, Alf Morris himself, although expressing some small satisfaction with the progress that had been made, was somewhat more circumspect. He, perhaps more than most, had the vision to recognise that his Chronically Sick and Disabled Persons Act 1970 was only the beginning of a revolution that would really change the world of disability and, particularly, discrimination against disabled people.

'The new Act has been most warmly welcomed by all the voluntary organisations working among handicapped people, but there is still much to do if we are to turn precept and law into administrative practice and full social provision,' he said then. 'The problem still facing us is a vast one requiring every organisation, statutory and voluntary alike, to discuss their priorities. We need a blueprint which provides for resources to be used as humanely and effectively as possible and to maximum efficiency in reducing the handicapping effects of disability.

'None of the very wide fellowship who helped to make and enact my Bill ever doubted the size and gravity of the task we confronted. Yet we hoped, by working together, that we could change the status quo for Britain's disabled and end the serene self satisfaction by which they were oppressed.'

The big problem was that provision was left to local authorities, and that there were still considerable differences in delivery. Although the Alf Morris Act made it mandatory for local authorities to improve welfare services, the actual delivery was patchy in the extreme.

For instance, Section 2 of the Act made mandatory these services:

Practical assistance for disabled people in their own homes.

Assistance for those who could not otherwise afford them to obtain radio and television facilities, and help to obtain library and other recreational facilities in disabled persons' own homes.

Provision of similar recreational facilities outside their homes and assistance with use of educational facilities.

Provision of travel facilities to enable participation in such recreational, educational or other similar facilities.

Assistance with home adaptations and the provision of additional facilities for the greater comfort, safety or convenience of disabled people at home.

Assistance in taking holidays.

Provision of meals, either in the home or elsewhere.

Assistance in obtaining telephones and any necessary special equipment for their use by disabled persons.

Surveys undertaken after the Act became law showed, however, that great gaps were still apparent between the enthusiastic local authorities and the most Scrooge-like. Those that were at the top in the provision they provided under the limited possibilities of the 1948 National Assistance Act, on the whole continued to be the most generous, whilst some others were also consistently near the bottom as they always had been. One of the problems was that the Act had made no provision for enforcement. It is doubtful in the first place whether the Tory Government which came into power had the political will to secure full implementation and, even if it had, it is difficult to see what they could actually do to local authorities who consistently performed badly.

However, it has to be stated that there was overall a huge increase in the numbers of individuals receiving help. The emphasis made by Section 1 of the Chronically Sick and Disabled Persons Act, that disabled people must be identified and recorded, meant that more people were made aware of their rights and the help they could receive, and this ensured an increase in those receiving help under the Act. In fact, the numbers of households identified as having a disabled member went up by almost two-thirds between 1972 and 1978.

New hope and expectations for disabled people came again in 1974 when the Labour Party was returned, and Alf Morris was immediately appointed as Britain's and, in fact, the world's, first Minister with special responsibility for the welfare of disabled people. The Queen's speech in 1974 made particular mention of new measures he would be bringing in to help disabled people. It has to be said that those local authorities who still managed not to admit need in individual cases managed to avoid facing up to their responsibilities, but that overall the Act brought immense benefits to the lives of disabled people and their families. Alf Morris set about dealing with the 'escape clauses' which enabled some local authorities to shirk their responsibilities.

There were many instances of the Act opening new doors which led to further enquiry and new leads to help disabled children and adults. A supreme example was the three sections on special education which placed duties on local education authorities towards deaf and blind, autistic and dyslexic children. With regard to autistic and dyslexic children, the Act officially established that such children existed, which previously many people in educational provision denied. The Act specified that their education should be arranged, as far as it was practicable, in schools maintained or assisted by the local education authority. This, in turn, led to a new focus on the requirement for the provision of special needs education. In 1974 Alf Morris set up a Committee of Inquiry chaired by Mary Warnock. As a direct result of its findings, published in May 1978, the Education Act 1981 and the Education Act 1993 added to the legislation which has so helped these children.

Housing specially built or adapted for disabled people was another emphasis of the Alf Morris Act. Implementation of this aspect had been slow to get off the ground. Only sixteen houses specially designed for disabled people were built in the first year and a half after the Act became law. However, by the end of 1978 over 3000 specially designed dwellings for wheelchair users had been built, and housing associations had joined the drive with 303 such houses with another 1000 under construction. Much of the increase in provision came after an Alf Morris circular about the need for local authorities to do more for housing disabled people or to help housing associations to do so. More importantly, it emphasised the fact that the needs of disabled people were not all the same. It had become obvious that the need for wheelchair-friendly housing was limited, but that there was a great deal of need for a variety of provision that helped those with other forms of physical disability.

Another aspect of Section 2 of the Chronically Sick and Disabled Persons Act had been the duty put upon local authorities to adapt existing housing to help disabled people. A great many adaptations were undertaken, but almost 90% of these cost under £150 each, giving an indication that some local authorities were still reluctant to take on more costly adaptations.

The 1978 Circular 59/78 on adaptations made it known in no uncertain terms that, although *both* housing and social services departments had the powers to adapt houses for disabled people, this should not be allowed to cause a delay in making these improvements. It then went on to define responsibilities: structural adaptations to private properties, like ramps, kitchen equipment, entryphones and handrails should be the task of housing departments; social services should undertake the task of enabling disabled people to get non-structural aids and for identifying and assessing needs for structural alterations. To prevent disabled people falling into the trap of having to pay more local rates on the improvement to their homes, Alf Morris brought in the Rating (Disabled Persons) Act which came into effect in April 1979.

Sections 4, 5 and 6 of the Chronically Sick and Disabled Persons Act were designed to encourage and assist disabled people to join in the day to day life of the community. Section 4 said that any new public building must make provision for disabled people in terms of access, toilets, the loop system and so on. Sections 4 and 5 dealt with adaptations to existing buildings to provide access. All these sections in the published Act contained a waiver that such access should be provided, 'as far as was both reasonable and practicable'. Although some progress was made whilst the Conservatives were in power this waiver clause made it inevitable that some local authorities and owners of buildings would evade their responsibilities.

Because he was aware of this, Alf Morris in June 1977 set-up the Silver Jubilee Access Committee, under the Chairmanship of Sir Peter Large, which reported in 1979 that there was thoughtless disregard for the needs of disabled people. It also said that many property developers claimed they were not aware of the access provisions in the Act. Where they admitted knowing about them, they expressed the belief that the waiver clauses allowed them not to pay heed. Some also used safety legislation, particularly that dealing with fires, to exclude disabled people from buildings.

On the whole, however, the committee expressed the view that slowness in making access available was not due to wilful disregard for disabled people but to ignorance, and concluded that increasing awareness of their access problems would result in more adaptations and more facilities in new buildings. In January 1979, guidelines were sent to all local authorities and other organisations recommending the establishment of local access committees and access officers. However the committee also worried about instances of discrimination against disabled people and recommended further investigations.

Accordingly one of the last actions Alf Morris undertook as Minister for Disabled People in 1979 was to appoint a new body to carry on the work of the Queen's Silver Jubilee Committee and 'to consider the architectural and social barriers which may discriminate against disabled people and prevent them from making full use of facilities available to the general public'. Known as the Committee On Restrictions Against Disabled People (CORAD), it took on an additional hue, as Alf Morris had hoped and provided for in his remit. It went beyond access and looked at the whole subject of discrimination. CORAD strongly recommended wider anti-discrimination legislation, similar to that designed to protect racial minorities, in order to 'prevent the unjustifiable withholding, whether intentional or not, of some service, facility or opportunity from a disabled person because of that person's disability'. It was an important moment. Thinking had moved beyond physical provision to subtler and deeper issues, which has since led to more far-reaching legislation to revolutionise the lives of disabled people.

Sir Peter Large was appointed also to chair CORAD and at its first meeting in April 1979 he said: 'Our job, as I see it, is to devise means of ensuring that in the future nobody has any excuse for discriminating against disabled people. Somehow we have to devise a means of preventing society riding roughshod over the rights of disabled people.'

There is no doubt at all that the Morris Act was crucially important. Although some campaigners were disappointed that the lives of disabled people had not suddenly become revolutionised overnight, most agreed that it was the starting pistol which began a long-distance race, still in progress, not only in the UK but throughout the world. As well as improving lives, the great publicity it received and the new awareness it created about disabled people, led to a higher perception of the issues. It also resulted in more disabled people being seen in the community – many of them in employment for the first time – bringing greater acceptance and realisation that more help was needed.

Moreover, although there had been some pessimism about the response of local authorities, the Morris Act led to a real increase in spending to meet the needs of disabled people, from £330 million in 1971-72 to £3.3 billion in 1981-82. Also, the Act enabled Alf Morris, directly after his appointment as the first Minister for Disabled people in 1974, to introduce four new cash benefits.

In 1975 came the Non-Contributory Invalidity Pension (NCIP), a benefit for people of working age who, because of inadequate or low insurance stamp contributions, did not qualify for Contributory Invalidity Benefit. It was paid to people who were incapable of work, and it was not means-tested or taxable. Those receiving it were also credited with national insurance contributions. However, groundbreaking advance though it was, the sum paid was only 60% of the full Contributory Invalidity Pension, and many still had to rely on Supplementary Benefit to bring income up to subsistence level. In 1975 a much lower level of NCIP became payable to people resident in hospitals for the mentally handicapped or mentally ill who had no contribution record. Under the 1959 Mental Health Act they could receive 'pocket money', but levels varied greatly from hospital to hospital. The introduction of a standard rate paid under the NCIP made the system much more just.

The same year saw the introduction of the Housewives' Non-Contributory Invalidity Pensions (HNCIP). A 1974 White Paper on benefits did not contain any commitment on a payment for this group of disabled people, but a revolt by backbench MPs during the committee stages of the Social Security Bill 1975 forced the Government to extend the payment of a non-contributory benefit to married women at home. However, it did not do so without creating complications. The Government said that because some married women chose not to work, disabled married women could not just be awarded the benefit. They would need to prove that they were incapable both of paid employment and of performing normal household duties to be able to claim. Because this household duties test brought with it administrative and assessment problems, the introduction of the Married Woman's Pension did not materialise until November 1977.

The Invalid Care Allowance – now the Carer's Allowance – which came out of the same 1974 White Paper, was introduced to help people of working age who would have been able to go out to work had it not been for the need to care for a disabled relative. It began to be paid in November 1975. Payment was dependent on the person cared for being in receipt of the Attendance Allowance. However, this benefit also came with a strange caveat: although most full-time carers were likely to be women, married women were not able to claim because they might be at home in any event. On the brighter side, recipients were credited with their National Insurance stamp which meant they would be entitled to a pension after retirement age.

These three benefits gave disabled people an income as of right for the first time ever. The other benefit introduced by Alf Morris was the Mobility Allowance. Like the Attendance Allowance, this was a non-contributory, non-means-tested benefit, and the first payments were made in January 1976. It was limited to people suffering from such physical disability that they were 'unable to walk or virtually unable to do so' who were between the ages of five and sixty-five. At the time it was introduced, the allowance was £5 a week.

Previously the National Health Act 1946 had allowed the provision of a developed version of the motorised bath chair created by the Red Cross after World War I. This was the dreaded, despised and dangerous invalid trike, a three-wheeler that snailed along roads causing frustration both for the disabled drivers themselves and their fellow motorists. The main drawback of the invalid car was that it was for solo use by disabled persons: it did not enable their wives, husbands, friends or children to join them in their vehicles. For a few people – disabled parents in sole charge of children or a disabled person who lived with a relative or was blind – a small car could be provided as an alternative to the trike. Those with vehicles were entitled to claim a £100 a year private car maintenance allowance.

This provision was made under the medical, nursing and other services required at or for the purposes of hospitals in the 1946 Act. It was only under the Health Service and Public Health Act 1968 that the Secretary of State was specifically authorised to provide vehicles for all people disabled enough to meet the criteria, but the vehicle available to disabled people was still the trike alone. There was a great deal of concern about its safety, and mounting pressure from voluntary organisations, led in April 1972, to the Secretary of State asking Lady Evelyn Sharp to 're-examine the limitations imposed upon persons whose mobility is reduced by severe physical disablement, not occasioned by old age, and the means by which those limitations can be mitigated, having regard to the needs and circumstances of the disabled people and to the help in cash or kind which the available resources permit or could permit from the various agencies with responsibilities for such persons'.

Her report was published in 1974. The greatest change suggested by Lady Sharp was that four-wheel cars and not invalid tricycles should be provided. In September 1974 the Government issued a statement titled 'Mobility for Disabled People: the Government's Intentions', which proposed what was to be called the Mobility Allowance, a weekly payment of £4.00 to replace the £100 a year private car allowance, but, unlike the private car allowance, payment of the Mobility Allowance would not depend on the ownership of or the ability to drive a car.

In November 1974, the Government asked the then Central Council for the Disabled to join a working party to advise on the arrangements for the Mobility Allowance. An interim report was made in August 1975, followed by a final report in May 1976. The legislation for the new allowance was contained in the Social Security Pensions Act 1975.

But how would its intentions be converted into providing cars for disabled people? The Central Council for the Disabled had looked at a scheme, but the snag was that a large capital sum was needed to set it up. However, during 1977, the Government invited Lord Goodman to investigate the manner in which the Mobility Allowance could be used to its best advantage. The result was the creation in December 1977 of a new organisation called Motability. They talked to car manufacturers and arranged discounts on vehicles, set-up a special insurance scheme, and arranged for the banks to register a company called Motability Finance Ltd, which had access to £100 million. This enabled Motability to buy cars and lease them out on very good terms to disabled people. The disabled person merely signed over the full amount of the Mobility Allowance. This worked very well, except for some people who had heavy initial conversion costs to make a car suitable to their needs and found it difficult to access these start-up capital sums. This was overcome in 1979 when Motability launched a hire-purchase scheme which could include the conversion costs. Motability also created a charitable fund to help disabled people who could still not afford the deposits on cars.

The Motability scheme, encouraged at all stages by Alf Ω as the Minister, was made a great success over the years by people like George Wilson, CBE, Director of RADAR, Sir Peter Large, Lord Sterling, and enthusiastic people at the Department of Transport's Motability Unit.

There were early problems, relating to the strict definition of the ability to walk and about who was entitled to the Mobility Allowance. There were, of course, other groups of disabled people, like the blind for instance, who have considerable problems with mobility. In 1978 the Royal Commission on Civil Liability and Compensation for Personal Injury promoted the cause of disabled children in particular who were excluded from the Mobility Allowance because of the walking definition. They recommended that the definition be reviewed so that children could be helped, including those who were overactive or mentally handicapped, who were technically mobile but whose mobility was subject to special difficulties. This was followed in 1979 by a new set of regulations which clarified inability to walk out doors to include people whose ability to do so was 'limited as to the distance over which or the speed at which or the length of time for which or the manner in which he can make progress on foot without severe discomfort'.

In an associated area of mobility for disabled people, Alf Morris also had a great deal to do with resolving the unsatisfactory situation regarding parking for disabled people who depended on cars to travel anywhere beyond the immediate surroundings of their own homes. During the nineteen sixties, a number of local authorities operated parking badge schemes to enable disabled drivers to park where other vehicles were not allowed to park. Unfortunately, the badges were only recognised in the areas in which they were issued so drivers had to apply for several badges. One widely travelled, well known disabled campaigner, "Denny" Denly, mounted some twenty or so badges on a board for display at his various destinations. A second and more serious drawback was that the badges were only available to disabled drivers; the needs of drivers of disabled passengers were ignored. This Alf Morris had corrected by Section 21 of Chronically Sick and Disabled Persons Act which provided for the provision of a badge of a 'prescribed form', which would be recognised throughout the country. And happily, as with the Mobility Allowance, was also available to disabled non-drivers.

The scheme's concessions have never applied in the City of London, the London Boroughs of Westminster and Kensington and Chelsea and part of the London Borough of Camden. Special traffic problems were said to preclude their joining. However, the London Borough of Islington, originally also outside the scheme, later joined without suffering disastrous parking problems. Changes to regulations in 1975 opened the scheme to blind people and extended concessions to badge holders by permitting vehicles displaying badges to park on single yellow lines for a maximum of 2 hours in England, Wales and Northern Ireland (in Scotland there is no time limit).

Overall, most commentators perceived the Alf Morris Act as

a giant step forward. As Mary Greaves, the distinguished disabled campaigner, put it:

'Governments – of both parties – have made significant benefits available to a large number of disabled people and it would be very difficult to argue that this has not been brought about by the discussion emanating from the Act which exposed the financial injustices and the serious plight of many families coping with disablement.'

Sir Peter Large, CBE, addressing the issue of mobility for disabled people, said:

'The Joint Committee on Mobility for Disabled people applauds the successful endeavours that led to the 1970 Act and Alf Morris's subsequent steadfast and tenacious efforts for disabled people. Looking back, the Act clearly made the public aware of the plight of disabled people for the first time. It put disabled people firmly on the map and established a foundation on which further progress could be soundly based. Even more significantly, perhaps, the Act was a charter for disabled people. It gave them a realistic sense of their importance and an understanding of their right to be citizens and participate fully in society.'

Peter Lainson, Chair of the Access Committee for England, said:

'The Chronically Sick and Disabled Persons Act was clearly intended to enable people to control effectively the management of their environment, but in practice perhaps its greatest influence has been in shaping much of the current social policy in our country.'

He went on:

'Section 4 of the Act required building owners to make provision for disabled people, and this in itself triggered formal improvements in access through planning and building regulations. Yet perhaps the greater impact has been the readiness today of people with disabilities to challenge the inadequate design of products, architectural standards and management systems. A tremendous amount has already been achieved in the promotion of universal, barrier-free design. The seeds of all this were sown by the Chronically Sick and Disabled Persons Act…'

Most of all the Act established that disabled people have rights, and has continuously ever since made it possible for organisations and individuals to pursue those rights. In the nineteen 'eighties', the provisions of the Chronically Sick and Disabled Persons Act were supplemented by other legislation. The Disabled Persons Act 1981, promoted by Dafydd Wigley, MP, provided beneficial additions to the main building regulations. These provided guidance on the requirements to enable disabled people to have access to new or substantially reconstructed non-domestic premises to which the public were to be admitted.

In 1986, the Act was strengthened by amending legislation to try to overcome the thorny issue of the patchy response to the provision of services by local authorities. Tom Clarke's Disabled Persons (Services, Consultation and Representation) Act extended Section 1 to make it mandatory for local authorities to produce more information relevant to the needs of disabled people. Section 2 of the Act was also strengthened by introducing a requirement for local authorities to assess the needs of disabled people when requested to do so by a disabled person or a carer. This Section was again strengthened in 1990 by Section (47) of the of National Health Service and Community Care Act making it mandatory for local authorities to assess the needs of people requiring community care services, to keep them informed about their rights, and to decide what services were needed without necessarily being requested to do so.

Chapter Fourteen

Discrimination and Rights

Alf Morris has maintained that there were three stages in the disability battle in the UK: access and mobility; benefits (income as of right); and human rights. The Chronically Sick and Disabled Persons Act started the journey towards access and mobility. Benefits followed in direct relationship to the needs brought out by the Act. And discrimination and rights began to be looked at as an issue when he set up the Committee On Restrictions Against Disabled People (CORAD), chaired by Sir Peter Large, in February 1979. This published its report in 1981, which was the first major call for anti-discrimination legislation. The report, importantly, highlighted the fact that discrimination was not just about being nasty to disabled people, but that the environmental design could in itself be discriminatory. The report brought some pressure on the Government to outlaw discrimination against disabled people but, unfortunately, the Tory Government of the day did not look favourably on it. It took another fourteen years to make real progress.

CORAD's report contributed in part to the drafting in 1991 of Alf Morris's Civil Rights (Disabled Persons) Bill, a watered down version of which led, four years later, to the Disability Discrimination Act 1995. The campaign and the lobbying to gain this legislation illustrated how much had changed for disabled people. Before the Chronically Sick and Disabled Persons Act little had altered for them over the centuries. They had no income as of right, they were isolated by the lack of access to community places, particularly places of entertainment and transport, they were forced to accept handouts so that the public regarded them as objects of charity and, worse still, as we have seen, even as objects of amusement.

In the nineteen seventies, eighties and nineties the climate of change brought about by the Morris Act encouraged disabled people to find their own voice. There was growing militancy, which surprised, even shocked, some people who still cherished the image of the charitable model of disability. On almost any issue related to their lives and rights disabled people now descended on Parliament, improved wheelchairs and motability cars now helping to get them there. Long gone were the days of waiting for the able-bodied to pick up the cudgel on their behalf. They had found their own voice, and a very vocal one. At the same time, many disabled people had also given deep consideration to the cultures and values of the disabled world. In most cases they have decided that they should be cherished as much as those of the rest of society. Deaf people, particularly, have developed a rich culture of their own using their methods of communication. In sport, events like the Paralympics have attracted a wide audience not only at the games themselves but through television. Blind people have developed their own sport and recreational activities.

As a direct result of the CORAD report and lobbying, the Disability Discrimination Act was passed, aimed at ending the persistent discrimination that disabled people still met in their day-to-day lives. It was the first legislation in the UK to deal with discrimination against disabled people. It provided protection in many areas of their lives such as employment, ability to access goods, facilities and services, and in the management, buying and renting of property or land. Some parts of the Act became law in December 1996, whilst others were introduced subsequently.

From December 1996 it became unlawful for service providers – businesses and organisations – to treat disabled people less favourably than other people for a reason related to their disability. From October 1999, they have also had to make reasonable adjustments for disabled people: for example, by providing additional help or making changes to the manner in which they provide their services, and may have to make reasonable adjustments to the physical features of their premises to remove physical barriers to disabled people.

The Act, importantly, also made it mandatory for schools, colleges and universities to provide information for disabled people, and allowed the Government to set minimum standards to help them to use public transport easily. To ensure that disabled people received their rights under the Disability Discrimination Act, the incoming Blair Government passed the Disability Rights Commission Act 1999 which established the Disability Rights Commission (DRC) as an independent body. Leading up to this further historic moment, in 1997 the Government announced its commitment to develop enforceable civil rights for disabled people. To make this become a reality it first established a ministerial task force to consult widely about how it should be achieved. Out of this the Government produced a White Paper with proposals on the role and functions of the Disability Rights Commission, based largely on the recommendations of the task force. There was a good response to the White Paper, and support for its objectives.

The Disability Rights Commission opened its doors on the 25th April 2000. The Special Educational Needs and Disability Act 2001 also amended the original Disability Discrimination Act of 1995. Bert Massie, CBE, was appointed as the first Chairman of the Disability Rights Commission. He is a man with a long record of campaigning for and serving disabled people, primarily through Rehabilitation International and the Royal Association for Disability and Rehabilitation (RADAR), first as Assistant Director and then, from 1990 until 1999, as its Director.

The Act describes the DRC's statutory duties as: working to eliminate discrimination against disabled people; promoting equal opportunities for them; encouraging good practice in their treatment; and advising the Government on the working of disability legislation.

Fleshing out this summary, it means that the DRC must assist disabled people to secure their rights and arrange for legal advice and help where needed. It had to disseminate information and advice to disabled people and their employers and service providers about their rights and duties under the Disability Discrimination Act. It has to prepare and review statutory codes of practice to provide practical guidance to employers and service providers on meeting their obligations under the DDA on good practice. It also has to provide an independent conciliation service in the event of disputes between disabled people and service providers over access to goods and services. The DRC has the duty also to undertake formal investigations into the treatment of disabled people in a particular organisation or sector, and into unlawful acts by them. Finally, it has the responsibility to undertake research to inform discussion and policy-making and to measure how well the law affecting the rights of disabled people is working.

Importantly, the Act gives a wide interpretation of disability. It describes a disabled person as 'anyone with a physical or mental impairment, which has a substantial and long-term effect on their ability to carry out normal day-to-day activities'. Within this broad statement, it further defines 'physical impairment' to include weakening or adverse change of a part of the body caused through illness, by accident or from birth. 'Mental impairment' is said to be those specifically mentioned in the WHO's 'International Classification of Diseases'.

The word substantial is further defined as not having to be too severe, but has to be more than minor or trivial. Long-term adverse effects are defined as those that have lasted, or are likely to last, more than twelve months. Normal day-to-today activity is given the meaning 'one that affects mobility; manual dexterity; physical co-ordination; continence; ability to lift, carry or otherwise move everyday objects; speech; hearing; eyesight; memory or ability to concentrate, learn or understand; or perception of the risk of physical danger'.

Part I of the Act deals with the meaning of 'disability' and 'disabled' person.

Part II covers employment; discrimination against applicants and employees; the meaning of 'discrimination'; the duty of the employer to make adjustments; exemption for small businesses.

Under enforcement, it gives guidance on: remedies and procedure; the validity of certain agreements; charities and support for particular groups of persons; advertisements suggesting that employers will discriminate against disabled persons.

Under the heading of 'discrimination by other persons', it deals with discrimination against contract workers; discrimination by trade organisations; the meaning of 'discrimination' in relation to trade organisations; the duty of trade organisations to make adjustments. In sections 16, 17 and 18, it covers alterations to premises occupied under leases; occupational pension schemes; and insurance services.

Part III highlights 'discrimination in other areas'.

Under 'goods, facilities and services', it defines the meaning of discrimination in this area, and the duty of providers to make adjustments. It also looks at discrimination in relation to premises; exemption for small dwellings going fully into enforcing these measures; and the importance of making advice and assistance available.

Part IV covers education at all levels – education of disabled persons, and their further and higher education.

Part V deals with public transport.

Under taxis, it creates new laws about taxi accessibility regulations; accessibility certificates; designated transport facilities; new licences conditional on compliance with taxi accessibility regulations; exemptions from such regulations; carrying persons in wheelchairs; carrying of guide dogs and hearing dogs; appeal against refusal of exemption certificate; requirements as to disabled passengers in Scotland.

The section on public service vehicles covers Public Service Vehicle Accessibility Regulations; accessibility certificates; approval certificates; special authorisations; reviews and appeals; and fees. It also establishes new Rail Vehicle Accessibility Regulations.

Part VI deals with the National Disability Council, and its code of practice.

Part VII is the 'supplemental' section and deals with such things as the codes of practice prepared by the Secretary of State; victimisation; help for persons suffering discrimination; aiding unlawful acts; liability of employers and principals; and statutory authority and national security.

Part VIII The last section of the Act, under the heading of Miscellaneous, addresses such areas as appointment by the Secretary of State of advisers; amendment of Disabled Persons (Employment) Act 1944; restriction of publicity in Industrial and Employment Appeal Tribunals; and financial provisions.

Now that they have, at last, got rights, disabled people have been far from slow in using or defending them. The DRC has already fought hundreds of cases of discrimination against disabled people, typically:

A youngster banned from a school trip because he had diabetes.

Ending of the employment of a local authority accountant with a history of clinical depression.

The refusal of entry to a man because of his facial disfigurement.

The repeated refusal of promotion on the grounds of deafness.

The failure to make reasonable adjustments to the post of a man with diabetes to allow him to continue as a roadworker.

For the thousands of disabled people who have already

sought the DRC's help and advice, it is obviously meeting a real need. However, at the time of writing there are strong indications that the days of its existence as a distinct organisation which exists to ensure that the rights of disabled people are met, may be numbered. It may be merged with organisations which exist to combat discriminations against other sections of the community.

Chapter Fifteen

The International Implications of the Morris Act

The Chronically Sick and Disabled Persons Act had wide implications for disabled people internationally. It was as if the world
had been waiting for a lead. The Act provided the guidelines and
impetus required for its principles and provisions for meeting
basic needs to be adopted in many other countries. The British
legislation was widely used as a model and some countries – after
the appointment of Alf Morris in 1974 – also appointed a
Minister for Disabled People. This in turn gave further impetus
to prioritising the needs of disabled people and improvements in
services and access.

However, the greatest world impact came from a Rehabilitation International initiative which relied on Alf Morris to achieve
its aims.

Because of the reputation his Act and his legislative achieve-
ments of his time as Minister for Disabled People gave him, he
was asked to chair the World Planning Group which – with a
highly distinguished membership drawn from the north, south,
east and west of the world – drafted Rehabilitation International's
Charter for the 1980s, the first-ever policy statement for disabled
people worldwide. This proclaimed the principles and priorities
that should guide policy-making internationally on disability. It
became the basis for the United Nations *World Programme of*

Action for disabled people and informed the General Assembly's decision to stage an International Year of the Disabled Person, two other major steps forward. The *Charter* was approved on 26 June 1980 by Rehabilitation International's 14th World Congress in Winnipeg.

The preamble set out the document's precise aims. *The Charter for the 1980s* was, it said, 'a statement of consensus about international priorities for action…' Its purposes were expressed in four aims supported by statements of general principles and recommended actions to translate them into reality. It was designed to promote the goals of 'full participation' and 'equality' for disabled persons throughout the world. This meant the right of every disabled person to share in the normal social life of the community in which he or she lives, and enjoy living conditions equal to those of other citizens, including an equal share in the improvement of standards of living resulting from social and economic development.

The drafting of the Charter was based on the most extensive international consultation ever undertaken in the field of disability prevention and rehabilitation. Issues to be included in the Charter were reviewed at national and regional meetings and conferences during the three-year period 1978-1980. They took place in every region of the world and closely informed the drafting of the charter en route to its approval at the World Congress.

Its 'Declaration' was bold and brave:

'More than 500 million people are disabled in the world today. In every country at least one person in ten is disabled by physical, mental or sensory impairment. They share the rights of all humanity to grow and learn, to work and create, to love and be loved, but they live in societies that have not yet learned to fully protect those rights for their citizens with disabilities. They are too often denied the opportunities and responsibilities which should be theirs.

'More than 350 million people with disabilities live without the help they need to enjoy a full life. They live in every nation, in every part of the world, but by far the greatest number live in areas at early stages of economic and social development. Here poverty joins with impairment to poison the hopes and diminish the lives of children, of adults and of families.

'An estimated 25% of the members of any community are prevented by the existence of disability from the full expression of their capacities. This includes not only people who are disabled, but also their families and others who assist and support them. Any society which fails to respond effectively to these problems accepts a huge loss of human resources and a cruel waste of human potential.

'Throughout history, humanity has erected barriers both physical and social which exclude from full participation in its communities those judged to be different because of physical or mental variations. Buildings and transportation are mostly inaccessible to people with disabilities. Information and art works of beauty do not reach those whose sight or hearing or comprehension is impaired. The warmth of human association is withheld from children and adults whose physical or mental capacities are different from those of the majority. Education, productive employment, public service, recreation and other human activities are denied to many or permitted only in segregation. For people with the most severe disabilities, who are unlikely ever to be capable of independent activity, there is often total neglect, or insufficient effort to assist their personal development and improve the quality of their lives.

'The knowledge and skills now exist to enable each country to remove the barriers which exclude people with disabilities from the life of its communities. It is possible for every nation to open all of its institutions and systems to all of its people. What is too often lacking is the political will to proclaim and translate into action the policies necessary to bring this about. A nation failing to respond to this challenge fails to realize its true worth.

'Poverty and war not only cause disability but also affect the availability of resources for its prevention and rehabilitation. The aims of this *Charter* require for their fulfillment, therefore, a more equitable distribution of the world's resources and relations between nations that are based on reason and co-operation.

'In the new decade it must be the goal of all nations to reduce the incidence of disability and to evolve societies which will respect the rights of persons with disabilities and welcome their full participation. For these purposes this *Charter for the 1980s* is promulgated. Its aims, each of importance and priority, can be achieved only when there is a basic modification of each society's attitude toward disability and of its response to the problems of disabled people,

The Aims are:

'To launch in each nation a programme to prevent as many impairments as possible, and to ensure that the necessary preventive services reach each family and every person.

'To make certain that every person with a disability, and every family which includes a member with a disability receives whatever rehabilitation services and other support and assistance may be needed to reduce the handicapping effects of disability and to make possible for each person a full life and constructive role in society.

'To take all necessary steps to ensure the fullest possible integration of and equal participation by people with disabilities in all aspects of the life of their communities.

'To disseminate information about people with disabilities and their potential, and about disability, its prevention and treatment, so as to increase public knowledge and awareness of these problems and of their importance in every society'.

In order to achieve these aims, the Charter went on:

'Each country is urged to prepare a comprehensive national plan for the achievement of these aims in the light of the principles enunciated in this Charter and its own circumstances. The plan should involve all major sectors of national life and be a component of high priority in any programmes for national development; it should provide for the full participation of people with disabilities in such programmes.

'It is essential for each country to have within its Government a Minister or an individual of senior rank, directly responsible to the Head of State or Government, as is appropriate, to direct the preparation of the national plan and to co-ordinate its implementation. This person should be assisted by a national advisory body including representatives of all relevant Government departments, organisations of people with disabilities, and voluntary and professional groups.

'*The Charter of the 1980s* is a statement of consensus about measures to enable humanity to protect and nourish the rights and responsibilities of every person, those who are called disabled and those who are not.'

It then went on to outline nine fundamental concepts which set the scene for action. The Charter spelt out, in sixty-two subsections, what action it demanded under each of its previously stated aims. Leaving absolutely nothing to chance, Alf Morris's steering group then came up with a masterly detailed list of targets for action in the 1980s:

'On the basis of the fundamental principles enunciated in this Charter, and recognising that the capability of nations to take actions for disability prevention and rehabilitation will vary according to their national priorities and the availability of the necessary resources, Rehabilitation International sets forth the following targets for action during the Decade of the 80s to service as a guideline and stimulus for all nations.

Targets at a community level:

Shifting of the focus of rehabilitation to the community level. This includes extension of community level rehabilitation services, in both urban and rural locales, and preferably within existing community services.

Strengthening all measures to foster community integration of people with disabilities including elimination of all barriers to their use of public facilities and services.

Establishment of a system within each community for early identification of children with disabilities.

Providing rehabilitation services to all in need of them without discrimination on the basis of age, sex, financial capability, religious or ethnic background, or type and cause of impairment.

Expanding training of community level personnel to identify people with disabilities, assist them and their families, and, when necessary, refer them to services and programmes appropriate to their needs. All generic training programmes for community workers, including teachers, social workers, health service personnel, administrators, clergy, family counsellors, and civic planners, should incorporate basic training about the nature of disability and the rehabilitation process.

Adopting of measures by trade unions and employers to facilitate employment of members of the community with disabilities. Employers of large numbers of workers, particularly agencies of Government, should be encouraged to take the lead.

Adopting of measures by trade unions and employers to prevent disability accidents at work and to reduce injuries to workers.

Targets at the national Level:

Reducing malnutrition and under-nutrition, particularly among young children, and women of child-bearing age.

Expanding programmes of immunization against the six major infectious diseases: poliomyelitis, tuberculosis, diphtheria, whooping cough, tetanus and measles.

Including measures for disability prevention within all national programmes for health, education and environmental control.

Enriching the training programmes for all categories of professional workers concerned with aspects of disability prevention and the rehabilitation process, including teachers, nurses, physicians, social workers, and governmental planners, to include comprehensive information on these subjects.

Providing within all national policies on education for adapted programmes and facilities integrated as far as possible to meet the needs of disabled children and adults with all types and extent of disability and including particularly the severely disabled person.

Reviewing existing educational policies to eliminate any provisions that discriminate against children and adults with disabilities.

Assuring increased availability of technical aids and devices for independent living and arranging exemption from customs duties and tariffs, and provision of import licences and foreign exchange allocations as needed to acquire these items.

Adoption by each nation of the Protocol providing for duty-free importation of articles needed by persons with disabilities to the UNESCO 'Florence Agreement' on importation of Educational, Scientific and Cultural Materials.

Developing simpler and less expensive methods for rehabilitation service delivery.

Examining existing systems of social security and social insurance to determine that they do not exclude or discriminate against people with disabilities and their families.

Examining existing conditions of employment to determine that people with disabilities engaged in work equal to that of other workers are not discriminated against as a result of disability with regard to wages and other conditions of employment.

Adopting measures to assure the place of people with disabilities in employment along with all other qualified and available workers.

Education of the public as to the causes and effects of disability and its prevention, the potential of people with disabilities for rehabilitation, and the services available within the nation to this end. Such efforts should raise community consciousness of the capabilities of people with disabilities to contribute to national political, economic, and social life.

Opening all systems of society to the participation and contribution of people with disabilities, including particularly all public facilities, housing, transportation, social and health services, educational and work opportunities, cultural and social life, sports and recreational facilities.

Creating a central source of information and barrier-free design for people with all types of disabilities.

Amending national design and construction standards to take into account the elements and requirement of barrier-free design as well as features to eliminate environmental hazards at home, at work and in traffic.

Promoting the use of the International Symbol for Access to identify buildings and facilities free of architectural barriers to people with disabilities.

Stimulating the development of organisations of people with disabilities.

Examining all legislation to remove any provisions which discriminate against the rights of people with disabilities and their families.

Including in existing legislation provisions to co-ordinate services for disability prevention and rehabilitation services in all national plans for social and economic developments and regarding such programmes as legitimate targets for development assistance.

Establishment of an office or appointment of an individual, directly responsible to the Head of State or Government, to have primary responsibility for developing and implementing a comprehensive plan for disability prevention and rehabilitation, and creation of a national advisory body to assist in planning and action.

Establishing a system for monitoring national progress during the decade to accomplish the aims and action targets set forth in the Charter.

Targets at a world level:

Expanding international efforts to reduce malnutrition and under-nutrition, particularly among infants, young children, and women of child-bearing age.

Expanding efforts to extend primary health care to all communities.

Promoting expanded programmes for immunisation against the six major infectious diseases, targeting for particular attention the eradication of poliomyelitis by the year 1990.

Strenghtening international standards and programmes for the prevention of accidents in the home, at work, and on the roads.

Stimulating a massive programme of public information concerning the fundamental causes of disability, its effects on people, its prevention, the possibilities for rehabilitation, and the importance of social factors in forestalling the handicapping effect of disabilities.

Strengthening the international co-operation in the exchange of information, technical experience and innovation in the fields of disability prevention and rehabilitation.

Increased international co-operation in the training of personnel engaged in rehabilitation activities.

Encouraging international co-operation in the marketing of technical aids and devices to increase the availability at lower costs.

Expanding the activities of UN agencies in disability prevention and rehabilitation, particularly at the regional level.

Ensuring the widest possible dissemination of *The Charter for the 1980s* and drawing attention to its message at all levels of Government to the individuals most directly concerned in each community.'

It was the most far-seeing and far-reaching document ever published on disability. Interestingly, its sections on discrimination and rights were more than a decade ahead of their time. They could have been written for the Disability Discrimination Act.

Twenty years later, Alf Morris, by then Lord Morris of Manchester, was asked to chair another steering group of world-renowned figures to draft a *Charter for the New Millennium.* They included Professor Stephen Hawking; Sir Harry Fang, then

President of Rehabilitation International; HRH Prince Ra'ad Bin Zeid of Jordan; Anatole Ossadchik, Minister for Social Affairs, Russian Federation; Archbishop Desmond Tutu; Justin Dart, then Chairman of the US President's Committee on the Employment of People with Disabilities; Deng Pufang, Chairman of the China Disabled Persons Federation; HE Chief Emeka Anyaoku, then Commonwealth Secretary-General; Shri D K Manavalan of India.

The new Charter was approved by the Governing Assembly of Rehabilitation International in London on the 9th September 1999. This document was later presented to Heads of Government throughout the world, and was accepted by the United Nations, and will influence thinking in the same way as the Morris 1970 Act and the *The Charter for the 1980s* had done.

In Britain Prime Minister Tony Blair welcomed the new Charter in July 2000, saying at a Downing Street reception that he believed that it would form the basis of a global consensus on priorities for disabled people for at least the next decade. He added a year later in the House of Commons that this absolutely remained the Government's view.

In a debate on the *Charter for the New Millennium* in the House of Lords in July 2000 timed to follow its presentation to the Prime Minister, Lord Morris commented:

'The new Charter updates its highly acclaimed predecessor of 20 years ago, whose impact can be seen in the statute books of countries across the world and which became the basis for the UN's World Programme of Action for the Decade of Disabled Persons. *The Charter for the 1980s* was about basic rehabilitation services; full representation for disabled people on all public bodies making decisions affecting their lives; equal opportunities in education and the workplace; a basic income; and access to the built environment in a world where most countries had no disability legislation of any kind. The new Charter is mainly about prevention and the civil rights of the world's currently 600 million people with physical, intellectual and sensory disabilities.

It lays out what still needs to be done, not only in Britain, but internationally. I do not deny that much has changed due largely to legislation in Britain that influenced the world – but there is still a long agenda of unmet need before we achieve a lasting impact, particularly in terms of saving people from preventable disabilities in poor and rich countries alike'

The watchwords now were prevention and rights. The Charter's key strategy was to ask states to support the promulgation of a UN Convention on the Rights of People with Disabilities, which has since been endorsed by the General Assembly.

The new Charter's other calls were for Governments to take the simple measures needed to prevent the easily preventable diseases which lead to widespread disability, and to achieve social equality and full civil rights for disabled people. The Charter asserted that in much of the world the problems of disabled living are multiplied by unmerited but still lawful discrimination against disabled people, and that very much more needed to be done in empowering disabled people, not simply for reasons of compassion but of enlightenment.

The abridged version of the *Charter for the New Millennium* states:

> 'We enter the Third Millennium determined that the human rights of each person in every society shall be recognised and protected. This Charter is proclaimed to translate this vision into reality.

> 'Basic human rights are still routinely denied to entire sectors of the world's population, including many of the now estimated 600 million children, women and men who have disabilities. We seek a world where equal opportunity for disabled people becomes a natural consequence of enlightened policies and legislation supporting full inclusion in, and access to, all aspects of society.

> 'Scientific and social progress in the twentieth Century has increased understanding of the unique and inviolate value of each life. Yet ignorance, prejudice, superstition and fear still govern much of society's response to disability. In the Third Millennium, we must accept disability as an ordinary part of the varied human condition.

'In developed and developing countries, throughout the world, segregation and marginalisation have placed disabled people on the lowest rung of the social and economic ladder. In the 21st century, we must insist on the same human and civil rights for people with disabilities as for everyone else.

'The twentieth Century has demonstrated that with invention and ingenuity it is possible to extend access to every resource of the community – the physical, social and cultural environments, transportation, information, technology, mass voting and worship. In the twenty first Century, we must extend this access from the few to the many, dismantling all environmental, electronic and attitudinal barriers to full inclusion in community life. With that access can come the stimulation of participation and leadership, warmth of fellowship, the glories of shared affection, and the beauties of the earth and universe.

'Every minute of every day, more and more children and adults are being added to the number of persons whose disabilities result from the failure to prevent preventable diseases and failure to treat treatable conditions. Global immunisation and other prevention strategies are no longer aspirations: they are practical and cost-effective possibilities. What is needed is the political determination, primarily of governments, to end this affront to humanity.

'Technological advances are theoretically bringing manipulation of the genetic components of life within human control. This introduces new ethical dimensions to the international dialogue about disability prevention. In the Third Millennium we must create policies that respect the dignity of all people and the inherent balance and benefits derived from the wide diversity among them.'

To achieve these aims, the Charter says:

'International programmes to assist economic and social development should require minimum accessibility standards in all infrastructure projects, including technology and communications, to ensure people with disabilities are fully included in the life of their communities.'

'Every nation should have on-going, country-wide programmes to reduce or prevent any risk that might lead to impairment, disability or handicap, as well as early treatment
programmes for children and adults who become impaired.'

All disabled people should have access to treatment, information about self-help techniques and, if needed, provision of
adaptive and appropriate technologies.

Every person with an impairment, and every family with a
disabled member, should receive the rehabilitation services
necessary to optimise mental, physical and functional well-
being, thus ensuring the capacity of the disabled individual to
manage a life as independently as any other citizen.

Disabled people should have a central role in planning their
own rehabilitation and support programmes. And disabled
people's organisations should be empowered with the necessary
resources to share responsibility in national planning for rehabilitation and independent living.

Community based rehabilitation should be widely promoted
nationally and internationally as an affordable and sustainable
approach to services.

Each nation must develop, with the participation of organisations of and for people with disabilities, a comprehensive plan
with clearly defined targets and timetables for implementing
the aims expressed in this Charter.

The Charter calls on member states to make the promulgation of a United Nations Convention on the Rights of People with
Disabilities as a key strategy to achieve these goals.

The authors concluded: 'In the Third Millennium, it must
become the goal of all nations to evolve into societies that protect
the rights of people with disabilities by supporting their full empowerment and inclusion in all aspects of life. For these purposes,
the *Charter for the Third Millennium* is proclaimed for action by
all states, in the conviction that the implementation of its aims is
a primary responsibility of each Government, and of all relevant
non-governmental and international organisations'.

What does the future hold for disabled people and the prevention of disability? Looking back before 1970, matters have improved enormously, but there is still much to be achieved, not least for the poorest countries. There is a division in the world. In Britain and the developed world there has been an awakening as societies and governments have faced up to some of their responsibilities. Elsewhere in the world the long journey is only just beginning and, because of poverty and the lack of political will, it will be a slow, hard and painful one. Ignorance, prejudice, superstition and fear still govern responses in many countries to this challenge. It is tragic that so many people still live with disabilities that are now easily preventable at very low cost. Four out of five of the world's millions of blind people live in developing countries, and up to two-thirds of blindness there is preventable, or routinely curable through cataract operations. Other types of disability, which are now preventable by good occupational health practice, are widespread. Still others are caused in many parts of the developing world by lack of such basic needs as clean water, adequate sewage treatment, reduction of over-crowding, a nourishing diet, and good medical attention.

The watchword for the future must be prevention. Those of us fortunate enough to live in countries which at least give half an ear and the corner of an eye to the needs and feelings of disabled people must take up the challenge and empower those who live in places where such feelings and needs are still ignored. If there is one lesson for humankind from this book, it is that this is a struggle not just for disabled people but for us all.

Chronically Sick and Disabled Persons Act 1970

ARRANGEMENT OF SECTIONS
– 'A humane and historic statute'

Welfare and housing
Section:
1. Information as to need and existence of welfare services.
2. Provision of welfare services.
3. Duties of Housing authorities.
   Premises open to public.
4. Access to, and facilities at, premises open to the public.
5. Provision of public sanitary conveniences.
6. Provision of sanitary conveniences at certain premises open to the public.
7. Signs at buildings complying with ss.4-6.
   University and school buildings
8. Access to, and facilities at, university and school buildings.
   Advisory committees, etc.
9. Central Advisory Committee on War Pensions.
10. Housing Advisory Committee.
11. National Insurance Advisory Committee.
12. Industrial Injuries Advisory Council.
13. Youth employment service.

14. Miscellaneous advisory committees.
15. Co-option of chronically sick or disabled persons to local authority committees.
16. Duties of National Advisory Council under Disabled Persons (Employment) Act 1944.
    Provisions with respect to persons under 65
17. Separation of younger from older patients.
18. Information as to accommodation of younger with older persons under welfare powers.
19. Provision of information relating to chiropody services.
    Miscellaneous provisions
20. Use of invalid carriages on highways.
21. Badges for display on motor vehicles used by disabled persons.
22. Annual report on research and development work.
23. War Pensions appeals.
24. Institute of Hearing research.
25. Special educational treatment for the deaf-blind.
26. Special educational treatment for children suffering autism, & c.
27. Special educational treatment for children suffering from acute dyslexia.
28. Power to define certain expressions.
29. Short title, extent and commencement.

An Act to make further provision with respect to the welfare of chronically sick and disabled persons; and connected purposes. [29th May 1970]

BE IT ENACTED by the Queen's most Excellent Majesty, by and with the advice of the Lords Spiritual and Temporal, and Commons, this present Parliament assembled, and by the authority of the same, as follows:

Welfare and housing

1.

(1) It shall be the duty of every local authority having functions under section 29 of the National Assistance Act 1948 to inform themselves of the number of persons to whom that section applies within their area and of the need for the making by the authorities of arrangements under the section for such persons.

Information as to need for and existence of welfare services.1948 c.29

(2) Every such local authority ---

(a) shall cause to be published from time to time at such times and in such manner as they consider appropriate general information as to the services provided under arrangements made by the authority under the said section 29 which are for the time being available in their area; and

(b) shall ensure that any such person as aforesaid who uses any of those services is informed of any other of those services which in the opinion of the authority is relevant to his needs.

(3) This section shall come into operation on such dates as the Secretary of State may by order made statutory instruments appoint.

2.

(1) Where a local authority having functions under section 29 of the National Assistance Act 1948 is satisfied in case of any person to whom this section applies who is ordinarily resident in their area that it is necessary to meet the needs of that person for that authority to make arrangements for all or any of the following matters, namely ---

Provision of welfare services.1948 c.29

(a) the provision of practical assistance for that person in his home;

(b) the provision for that person of, or assistance to that person in obtaining, wireless, television, library or similar recreational facilities;

(c) the provision for that person of lectures, games, outings or other recreational facilities outside his home or assistance to that person in taking advantage of educational facilities available to him;

(d) the provision for that person of facilities for, or assistance in, travelling to and from his home for the purpose of participating in any services provided under arrangements made by the authority under the said section 29 or, with the approval of the authority, in any services provided otherwise than as aforesaid which are similar to services which could be provided under such arrangements;

(e) the provision of assistance for that person in arranging for the carrying out of any works of adaptation in his home or the provision of any additional facilities designed to secure his greater safety, comfort or convenience.

(f) facilitating the taking of holidays by that person, whether at holiday homes or otherwise and whether provided under arrangements made by the authority or otherwise;

(g) the provision of meals for that person whether in his home or elsewhere;

(h) the provision for that person of, or assistance to that person in obtaining, a telephone and any special equipment necessary to enable him to use a telephone, then, not withstanding anything in any scheme made by the authority under the said section 29, but subject to the provisions of section 35(2) of that Act (which requires local authorities to exercise their functions under Part III of that Act under the general guidance of the Secretary of State and in accordance with the provisions of any regulation made for the purpose), it shall be the duty of that authority to make these arrangements in exercise of their functions under the said section 29.

(2) Without prejudice to the said section 35(2), subsection (3) of the said section 29 (which requires any arrangements made by a local authority under that section to be carried into effect

in accordance with a scheme made thereunder) shall not apply ---

(a) to any arrangements made in pursuance of subsection (1)of this section; or

(b) in the case of a local authority who have made such a scheme, to any arrangements made by virtue of subsection (1) of the said section 29 in addition to those required or authorised by the scheme which are so made with the approval of the Secretary of State.

3.

(1) Every local authority for the purposes of Part V of the Housing Act 1957 in discharging their duty under section 91 of that Act to consider housing conditions in their district and the needs of the district with respect to the provision of further housing accommodation shall have regard to the special needs of chronically sick or disabled persons; and any proposals prepared and submitted to the Minister by the authority under that section for the provision of new houses shall distinguish any houses which the authority propose to provide which make special provision for the needs of such persons.

Duties of housing authorities.1957 c.56

(2) In the application of this section to Scotland for the words 'Part V of the Housing Act 1957', '91' and 'Minister' shall be substituted respectively the words 'Part VII of the Housing (Scotland) Act 1966', '137' and 'Secretary of State'.

1966 c.49

Premises open to public

4.

(1) Any person undertaking the provision of any building or premises to which the public are to be admitted, whether on payment or otherwise, shall, in the means of access both to and within the building or premises, and in the parking facilities and sanitary conveniences to be available (if any), make provision, in so far as in the circumstances both practicable and reasonable, for the needs of members of the public

visiting the building or premises who are disabled.

Access to, and facilities at, premises open to the public.

(2) This section shall not apply to any building or premises intended for purposes mentioned in subsection (2) of section 8 of this Act.

5.

(1) Where any local authority undertakes the provision of a public sanitary convenience, it shall be the duty of the authority, in doing so, to make provision, in so far as it is in the circumstances both practicable and reasonable, for the needs of disabled persons.

Provision of public sanitary conveniences.

(2) Any local authority which in any public sanitary convenience provided by them make or have made provision for the needs of disabled persons shall take such steps as may be reasonable, by sign-posts or similar notices, to indicate the whereabouts of the convenience.

(3) In this section 'local authority' means a local authority within the meaning of the Local Government Act 1933 or the Local Government (Scotland) Act 1947 and any joint board or joint committee of which all the constituent authorities are local authorities within the meaning of either of those Acts.1933 c.51 1947 c.43

6.

(1) Any person upon whom a notice is served with respect to any premises under section 89 of the Public Health Act (which empowers local authorities by notice to make requirements as to the provision and maintenance of sanitary conveniences for the use of persons frequenting certain premises used for the accommodation, refreshment or entertainment of members of the public) shall in complying with that notice make provision, in so far as it is in the circumstances both practicable and reasonable, for the needs of persons frequenting those premises who are disabled.1936 c.49

(2) The owner of a building, who has been ordered under section 11 (4) of the Building (Scotland) Act 1959 to make the

building conform to a provision of building standards regulations made under section 3 of that Act requiring the provision of suitable and sufficient sanitary conveniences therein, shall in complying with that order make provision, in so far as it is in the circumstances both practicable and reasonable, for the needs of persons frequenting that building who are disabled.1959 c.24

7.

(1) Where any provision required by or under section 4, 5 or 6 of this Act is made at a building in compliance with that section, a notice or sign indicating that provision is made for the disabled shall be displayed outside the building or so as to be visible from outside it.

Signs at buildings complying with ss.4-6.

(2) This section applies to a sanitary convenience provided elsewhere than in a building, and not itself being a building, as it applies to a building.

University and school buildings

8.

(1) Any person undertaking the provision of a building intended for the purposes mentioned in subsection (2) below shall, in the means of access both to and within the building, and in the parking facilities and sanitary conveniences to be available, be both practicable and reasonable, for the needs of persons using the building who are disabled.

Access to, and facilities at, university and school buildings.

(2) The purposes referred to in subsection (1) above are the purposes of any of the following:

   (a) universities, university colleges and colleges, schools and halls of universities;

   (b) schools within the meanings of the Education Act 1944, teacher training colleges maintained by local education authorities in England and Wales and other institutions providing further education pursuant to a scheme under section 42 of that Act;1944 c.31

   (c) educational establishments within the meaning of the

Education (Scotland) Act 1962. 1962 c.37

Advisory commitments, etc

9.

(1) The Secretary of State shall ensure that the Central Advisory Committee constituted under section 3 of the War Pensions Act 1921 includes the chairmen of not less than twelve of the committees established by schemes under section 1 of that Act and includes at least one war disabled pensioner, and shall cause that Central Advisory Committee to be convened at least once every year. Central Advisory Committee on War Pensions. 1921 c.49

(2) This section extends to Northern Ireland.

10. In the appointment of persons to be members of the Central Housing Advisory Committee set up under section 143 of the Housing Act 1957 or the Scottish Housing Advisory Committee set up under section 167 of the Housing (Scotland) Act 1966, regard shall be had to the desirability of that Committee's including one or more persons with the knowledge of the problems involved in housing the chronically sick and disabled and to the person or persons with that knowledge being or including a chronically sick or disabled person or persons.

Housing Advisory Committees. 1957 c.56 1966 c.49

11. The National Insurance Advisory Committee shall include at least one person with experience of work among and of the needs of the chronically sick and disabled and in selecting any such person regard shall be had to the desirability of having a chronically sick or disabled person.

National Insurance Advisory Committee.

12. The Industrial Injuries Advisory Council shall include at least one person with experience of work among, and of the needs of, the chronically sick and disabled and in selecting any such person regard shall be had to the desirability of having a chronically sick or disabled person.

Industrial Injuries Advisory Council.

13.

(1) Without prejudice to any other arrangements that may be made by the Secretary of State, the Central Youth Employment Executive shall include at least one person with special responsibility for the employment of young disabled persons.

Youth employment service.

(2) In the appointment of persons to be members of any of the bodies constituted in pursuance of section 8(1) of the Employment and Training Act 1948 (that is to say, the National Youth Employment Council and the Advisory Committees on Youth Employment Council and the Advisory Committees on Youth Employment for Scotland and Wales respectively) regard shall be had to the desirability of the body in question including one or more persons with experience of work among, and the special needs of, young disabled persons and to the person or persons with that experience being or including a disabled person or persons. 1948 c.46

14.

(1) In the appointment of persons to be members of any of the following advisory committees or councils, that is to say, the Transport Users' Consultative Committees, the Gas Consultative Councils, the Electricity Consultative Councils, the Post Office Users' Consultative Councils and the Domestic Cost Consumers' Council, regard shall be had to the desirability of the Committee or Council in question including one or more persons with experience of work among, and the special needs of, disabled persons and to the person or persons with that experience being or including a disabled person or persons.

Miscellaneous advisory committees.

(2) In this section the reference to the Post Office Users' Councils is a reference to the Councils established under section 14 of the Post Office Act 1969, and in relation to those Councils this section shall extend to Northern Ireland.1969 c.48

15.

Where a local authority within the meaning of the Local Government Act 1933 or the Local Government (Scotland) Act 1947 appoint a committee of the authority under any enactment, and the members of the committee include or may include persons who are not members of the authority, then in considering the appointments to the committee of such persons regard shall be had, if the committee is concerned with matters in which the chronically sick or disabled have special needs, to the desirability of appointing to the committee persons with experience of work among, and of the needs of, the chronically sick and disabled, and to the person or persons with that experience being or including a chronically sick or disabled person or persons or co-option of chronically sick or disabled persons to local authority committees. 1933 c.51 1947 c.43

16.

The duties of the National Advisory Council established under section 17(1)(a) of the Disabled Persons (Employment) Act 1944 shall include in particular the duty of giving to the Secretary of State such advice as appears to the Council to be necessary on the training of persons concerned with---

(a) placing disabled persons in employment; or

(b) training disabled persons for employment.

Duties of National Advisory Council under Disabled Persons (Employment) Act 1944. 1944 c.10

Provisions with respect to persons under 65

17.

(1) Every Board constituted under section 11 of the National Health Service Act 1946 (that is to say, every Regional Hospital Board and every Board of Governors of a teaching hospital) and every Regional Hospital Board constituted under section 11 of the National Health Service (Scotland) Act 1947 shall use their best endeavours to secure that, so far as practicable, in any hospital for which they are responsible a person who is suffering from a condition of chronic illness or disability and who

(a) is in hospital for the purpose of long-term care for that condition; or

(b) normally resides elsewhere but is being cared for in the hospital because---

(i) that condition is such as to preclude him from residing elsewhere without the assistance of some other person; and

(ii) such assistance is for the time being not available, is not cared in the hospital as an in-patient in any part of the hospital which is normally used wholly or mainly for the care of elderly persons, unless he is himself an elderly person.

Separation of younger from older patients. 1946 c.81 1947 c.27

(2) Each such Board as aforesaid shall provide the Secretary of State in such form and at such times as he may direct with such information as he may from time to time require as to any persons to whom subsection (1) of this section applied who, not being elderly persons, have been cared for in any hospital for which that Board is responsible in such a part of the hospital as is mentioned in that subsection; and the Secretary of State shall in each year lay before each House of Parliament such statement in such form as he considers appropriate of the information obtained by him under this subsection.

(3) In this section 'elderly person' means a person who is aged sixty-five or more or is suffering from the effects of premature ageing.

18.

(1) The Secretary of State shall take steps to obtain from local authorities having functions under Part III of the National Assistance Act 1948 information as to the number of persons under the age of 65 appearing to the local authority in question to be persons to whom section 29 of that Act applies for whom residential accommodation is from time to time provided under section 21 (1) (a) or 26(1) (a) of that Act at any premises in a part of those premises in which such accommodation is so provided for persons over that age.

Information as to accommodation of younger with older persons under Part III of National Assistance Act 1948. 1948 c.29.

(2) The Secretary of State shall take steps to obtain from local authorities having functions under the Social Work (Scotland) Act 1968 information as to the number of persons under the age of 65 who suffer from illness or mental disorder within the meaning of section 6 of the Mental Health (Scotland) Act 1960 or are substantially handicapped by any deformity or disability and for whom residential accommodation is from time to time provided under section 59 of the said Act of 1968 at any premises in a part of those premises in which such accommodation is so provided for persons over that age. 1968 c.49 1960 c.61

(3) Every local authority referred to in this section shall provide the Secretary of State in such form and at such times as he may direct with such information as he may from time to time require for the purpose of this section; and the Secretary of State shall in each year lay before each House of Parliament such statement in such form as he considers appropriate of the information obtained by him under this section.

19.

Every local health authority empowered to provide chiropody services under section 12 of the Health Services and Public Health Act 1968, or under section 27 of the National Health Service (Scotland) Act 1947, shall provide the Secretary of State in such form and at such times as he may direct with information as to the extent to which those services are available and used for the benefit of disabled persons under the age of sixty-five. Provision of information relating to chiropody services. 1968 c.46. 1947 c.27

Miscellaneous provisions

20.

(1) In the case of a vehicle which is an invalid carriage complying with the prescribed requirements and which is being used in accordance with the prescribed conditions---

Use of invalid carriages on highways.

   (a) no statutory provision prohibiting or restricting the use of footways shall prohibit or restrict the use of that vehicle on a footway;

(b) if the vehicle is mechanically propelled, it shall be treated for the purposes of the Road Traffic Act 1960, the Road Traffic Act 1962, the Road Traffic Regulation Act 1967 and Part I of the Road Safety Act 1967 as not being a motor vehicle; and 1960 c.16 1962 c.59 1967 c.76 1967 c.30

(c) whether or not the vehicle is mechanically propelled, it shall be exempted from the requirements of the Road Transport Lighting Act 1957.1957 c.51.

(2) In this section 'footway' means a way which is a footway, foot path or bridleway within the meaning of the Highways Act 1959; and in its application to Scotland means a way over which the public has a right of passage on foot only or a bridleway within the meaning of section 47 of the Country-side (Scotland) Act 1967;1959 c.25 1967 c.86; 'invalid carriage' means a vehicle, whether mechanically propelled or not, constructed or adapted for use for the carriage of one person, being a person suffering from some physical defect or disability;'prescribed' means prescribed by regulations made by the Ministry of Transport;'statutory provision' means a provision contained in, or having effect under, any enactment.

(3) Any regulations made under this section shall be made by statutory instrument, may make different provision for different circumstances and shall be subject to annulment in pursuance of a resolution of either House of Parliament.

21.

(1) There shall be a badge of a prescribed form to be issued by local authorities for motor vehicles driven by, or used for the carriage of, disabled persons; and---

(a) subject to the provision of this section, the badge so issued for any vehicle or vehicles may be displayed on it or on any of them either inside or outside the area of the issuing authority; and

(b) any power under section 84C of the Road Traffic Regulation Act 1967 (which was inserted by the Transport Act 1968) to make regulations requiring that orders under the Act shall include exemptions shall be taken to extend the requiring that an exemption be given with reference to badges issued by one authority shall be given also with reference to badges issued by other authorities.

Badges for display on motor vehicles used by disabled persons. 1967 c. 76 1968 c.73

(2) A badge may be issued to a disabled person of any prescribed description resident in the area of the issuing authority for one or more vehicles which he drives and, if so issued, may be displayed on it or any of them at times when he is the driver.

(3) In such cases as may be prescribed, a badge may be issued to a disabled person of any prescribed description so resident for one or more vehicles used by him as a passenger and, if so issued, may be displayed on it or any of them at times when the vehicle is being used to carry him. A badge may be issued to the same person both under this subscription and under subscription (2) above.

(4) A badge may be issued to an institution concerned with the care of the disabled for any vehicle kept in the area of the issuing authority and used by or on behalf of the institution to carry disabled persons of any prescribed description; and any badge so issued may be displayed on the vehicle for which it is issued at times when the vehicle is being so used.

(5) A local authority shall maintain a register showing the holders of badges issued by the authority under this section, and the vehicle or vehicles for which each of the badges is held; and in the case of badges issued to disabled persons the register shall show whether they were, for any motor vehicle, issued under subsection (2) or under subsection (3) or both.

(6) A badge issued under this section shall remain the property of the issuing authority, shall be issued for such period as may be prescribed, and shall be returned to the issuing authority in such circumstances as may be prescribed.

(7) Anything which is under this section to be prescribed by regulations made by the Minister of Transport and Secretary of State by statutory instrument, which shall be subject to annulment in pursuance of a resolution of either House of

Parliament; and regulations so made may make provision---

(a) as to the cases in which authorities may refuse to issue badges, as to the fee (if any) which an authority may charge for the issue or re-issue of a badge; and

(b) as to the continuing validity or effect of badges issued before the coming into force of this section in pursuance of any scheme having effect under section 29 of the National Assistance Act 1948 or any similar scheme having effect in Scotland; and

(c) as to any transitional matters, and in particular the application to badges issued under this section of orders made before it comes into force and operating with reference to any such badges are referred to in paragraph (b) above (being orders made, or having effect as if made, under the Road Traffic Regulation Act 1967).1948 c.29 1967 c.76

(8) The local authorities for purposes of this section shall be the common council of the City of London, the council of a county or county borough in England and Wales or a London Borough and the council of a county or large burgh in Scotland; and in this section 'motor vehicle' has the same meaning as in the Road Traffic Act 1967.

(9) This section shall come into operation on such date as the Minister of Transport and the Secretary of State may by order made by statutory instrument appoint.

22.

The Secretary of State shall as respects each year lay before Parliament a report on the progress made during that year in research and development work carried out by or on behalf of any Minister of the Crown in relation to equipment that might increase the range of activities and independence or well-being of disabled persons, and in particular such equipment that might improve the indoor and outdoor mobility of such persons.

Annual report on research and development work.

23.

(1) The Pensions Appeal Tribunal Act 1943 shall have effect with the amendments specified in the subsequent provision of this section.

War pensions appeals. 1943 c.39.

(2) In section 5---

    (a) so much of subsection (1) as prevents the making of an appeal from an interim assessment of the degree of a disablement before the expiration of two years from the first notification of the making of an interim assessment (that is to say, the words from 'if; to 'subsection' where first occurring, and the words 'in force at the expiration of the said period of two years') is hereby repealed except in relation to a claim in the case of which the said first notification was given before the commencement of this Act;

    (b) in the second paragraph of the subsection (1) (which defines 'interim assessment' for the purposes of that subsection), for the words 'this subsection' there shall be substituted the words 'this section';

    (c) in subsection (2) (which provides for an appeal to a tribunal from a ministerial decision or assessment purporting to be a final settlement of a claim) at the end there shall be added the words 'and if the Tribunal so set aside the Minister's decision or assessment they may, if they think fit, make such interim assessment of the degree or nature of the disablement, to be in force until such date not later than two years after the making of the Tribunal's assessment, as they think proper';

    (d) subsection (3) (which makes provision as to the coming into operation of section 5) is hereby repealed.

(3) In section 6, after subsection (2) there shall be inserted the following subsection---

    (2A) Where, in the case of such a claim as is referred to in section 1,2,3 or 4 of this Act---

    (a) an appeal has been made under that section to the Tribunal and that appeal has been decided (whether with or without an appeal under subsection (2) of this section from the Tribunal's decision); but

(b) subsequently, on an application for the purpose made in like manner as an application for leave to appeal under the said subsection (2) jointly by the appellant and the Minister it appears to the appropriate authority (that is to say, the person to whom under the rules made under the Schedule to this Act any application for directions on any matter arising in connection with the appeal to the Tribunal fell to be made)to be proper so to do---

(i) by reason of the availability of additional evidence; or

(ii) except where an appeal from the Tribunal's decision has been made under the said subsection (2), on the ground of the Tribunal's decision being erroneous in point of law, the appropriate authority may, if he thinks fit, direct that the decision on appeal to the Tribunal be treated as set aside and the appeal from the Minister's decision be heard again by the Tribunal.

(4) In subsection (3) of section (6) (under which, subject to subsection (2) of that section, a tribunal's decision is final and conclusive) for the words 'subject to the last foregoing subsection' there shall be substituted the words 'subject to subsections (2) and (2A) of this section'.

(5) In consequence of the Secretary of State for Social Services Order 1968, in section 12(1), for the definition of 'the Minister' there shall be substituted the following:

"the Minister" means 'the Secretary of State for Social Services'.

S.I. 1968/1699

(6) This section extends to Northern Ireland.

24.

The Secretary of State shall collate and present evidence to the Medical Research Council on the need for an institute of hearing research, such institute to have the general function of co-ordinating and promoting research on hearing and assistance to the deaf and hard of hearing.

Institute of hearing research.

25.

(1) It shall be the duty of every local education authority to provide the Secretary of State at such times as he may direct with information on the provision made by that local education authority of special educational facilities for children who suffer the dual handicap of blindness and deafness.

Special educational treatment for the deaf-blind.

(2) The arrangements made by a local education authority for the special educational treatment of the deaf-blind shall, so far as is practicable, provide for the giving of such education in any school maintained or assisted by the local education authority.

(3) In the application of this section to Scotland for any reference to a local education authority there shall be substituted a reference to an education authority within the meaning of section 145 of the Education (Scotland) Act 1962. 1962 c.47

26.

(1) It shall be the duty of every local education authority to provide the Secretary of State at such times as he may direct with information on the provision made by that local authority of special educational facilities for children who suffer from autism or other forms of early childhood psychosis.

Special educational treatment for children suffering from autism, & c.

(2) The arrangements made by a local education authority for the special educational treatment of children suffering from autism and other forms of early childhood psychosis shall, so far as is practicable, provide for the giving of such education in any school maintained or assisted by the local authority.

(3) In the application of this section to Scotland for any reference to a local education authority there shall be substituted a reference to an education authority within the meaning of section 145 of the Education (Scotland) Act 1962.

27.

(1) It shall be the duty of every local education authority to provide the Secretary of State at such times as he may direct with information on the provision made by that local education authority of special educational facilities for children who suffer from acute dyslexia.

Special educational treatment for children suffering from acute dyslexia.

(2) The arrangements made by a local education authority for the special educational treatment of children suffering from acute dyslexia shall, so far as is practicable, provide for the giving of such education to any school maintained or assisted by the local education authority.

(3) In the application of this section to Scotland for any reference to a local education authority there shall be substituted a reference to an education authority within the meaning of section 145 of the Education (Scotland) Act 1962.

28.

Where it appears to the Secretary of State to be necessary or expedient to do so for the proper operation of any provision in this Act, he may by regulations made by statutory instrument, which shall be subject to annulment in pursuance of a resolution of either House of Parliament, make provision as to the interpretation for the purposes of that provision of any of the following expressions appearing therein, that is to say, 'chronically sick', chronic illness', 'disabled', and 'disability'.

Power to define certain expressions.

29.

(1) This Act may be cited as the Chronically Sick and Disabled Persons Act 1970.

Short title, extent and commencement.

(2) Section 1 and 2 of this Act do not extend to Scotland.

(3) Save as otherwise expressly provided by sections 9,14, and 23, this Act does not extend to Northern Ireland.

(4) This Act shall come into force as follows:

(a) sections 1 and 21 shall come into force on the day

appointed thereunder;

(b) sections 4,5,6,7, and 8 shall come into force at the expiration of six months beginning with the date this Act is passed;

(c) the remainder shall come into force at the expiration of three months beginning with that date.

Bibliography and further reading

Aktion T4, Heidritch
A Mosaic of Victims, Yitzhak Berenbaum
Ancient Medicine, Owsei Temkin and Lilian Temkin
Architects of Genocide, Richard Breitman

Bartholomew Fair, William Wordsworth
Be It Enacted, A.Darnbrough and D.Kinrade
By Trust Betrayed, Hugh Gallagher

Care, Cure, and Education of the Crippled Child, Henry Edward
    Abt
Charter for the 80s, Rehabilitation International
Charter for the Third Millenium, Rehabilitation International
Children of Hippocrates, Jack Booler
Civilisation and Disease, H.E.Sigerist
Closing the Asylum, Peter Barham
Condition of the Working Classes, Friedrich Engels

Disability and Society, emerging issues, Len Barton
Disability Discrimination Act 1995, Dept Education and
    Employment
Disability: Legislation and Practice. Cooke, Darnbrough,
    Glendinning, Greaves, Guthrie, Morris, Hilditch, Keeble,
    Kinrade, Stokes and Whitehead.
Disability Politics, Campbell and Oliver

Disability Reader-social sciences perspective, Tom Shakespeare
Disabled People in Britain and Discrimination, C.Barnes
Disabled We Stand, A.T.Sutherland
Disabling Barriers – Enabling Environments, J.Swain,
    V.Finkelstein, S.French and M.Oliver.
Disabling Policies? G.Fulcher
Diseases of Occupation, Raffle. Lee, McCallum, Murray
Directory for Disabled People, Ann Darnburgh and Derek
    Kincade
Discharged from Mental Hospitals, Phillip Bean and Patricia
    Mind
Doctors and Diseases in the Roman Empire, O.K.Norman
Doctors Under Hitler, Michael H Kater
Dr Johnson's London, Liza Pound

Early Medieval Medicine, L.C. MacKinney
East End 1888, W.Fishman
Egyptian Medicine, Carole Reeves
Employment Rights – Disability, Richard Painter and Keith Puttick
English Social History, G.M. Trevelyan
Entertainment in The Parisian Fairs in the Eighteenth Century,
    R.Isherwood, *Journal of Modern History*
Experiences of an Asylum Doctor, M.Lomax
Extraordinary Bodies, Rosemarie Garland Thomson

*From Curiosity to Prop: a note of the changing cultural significance
    of dwarves' presentations in Britain*, Carmeli, Yoram

Germany Executes Her Unfit, Michael Straight
Greatest Benefit To Mankind, Roy Porter
Guide to the Mental Deficiency Act, 1913, J.Wormald and
    S.Wormald

Handicapped and Impaired in Great Britain. A.Harris
Handicap in a Social World, A.Brechin, P.Liddiard and J.Swain.
Hansard

Historical Background of Industrial and Occupational Diseases,
H.E.Sigerist
History of Childhood and Disability, Philip Safford and E.
Safford
History of Disability, Henri-Jacques Stiker
History of Medicine, Brian Inglis
History of Medicine, Henry Sigerist
History of Miners Diseases, G.Rosen
Holocaust, Ed.O.Bartov
House of Commons Select Committee debates
Hygiene, Diseases and Mortality of Occupation, Percival

Independent Lives, J.Morris
International Classification of Handicaps and Incapacity,
Professor Philip Wood
Implementation of the Chronically Sick and Disabled Persons Act,
National Fund for Research Into Crippling Diseases

Life and Work of Sigmund Freud, E.Jones
Lunacy, Law and Conscience, K.Jones

Man Outside, B.Breed
Masters of Bedlam, A.Scull
Mental Health and Social Policy, K.Jones
Mobility of Physically Disabled People, HMSO 1974
Murderous Science, Benno Mueller-Hill

No Feet to Drag, A.Butler and A.Morris
Nazi Doctors, Robert Lifton

Permission to Destroy Life Unworthy of Life (Die Freigabe der
Vernichtung Lebensunwerten Leben), A.Hoche and
K.Binding.
Politics, Aristotle
Politics of Disablement, M.Oliver
Poverty in the United Kingdom, P.Townsend

Provision for the Disabled, E.Topliss

Racial Hygiene, Robert Proctor
Raw Material: Producing Pathology in Victorian Culture,
    E.O'Connor
Reframing the Freak, Kochanek, *Victorian Periodicals Review*
Report on the Working Party on Mobility Allowance, Central
    Council for the Disabled
Registered as Disabled, S. Sainsbury
Removing Disabling Barriers, G.Zarb
Right to Death (Das Recht auf den Tod), A.Jost
Believe It or Not, Ripley's
Rise and Fall of the Sideshow Alley, R.Broome, Australian
    Historical Studies

Sexuality and Disability, Elaine Cooper

Telepathy, The Elephant Man, Monstration, J.McKenzie. *Journal
    of Popular Culture*
The Republic, Plato
Therapy of the World in Classical Antiquity, L.J.Rather and John
    Sharp
Town Labourer, L.B Hammond
Tragedy of Children Under Nazi Rule, Kiryl Sosnowski

Understanding Disability, M.Oliver

Water Babies, C.Kingsley
Wild Tribes of London, Phillip Watts

Index

Also available from
New European Publications

CHILDSCOURT

John Coleman

Foreword by Nigel Whiskin MBE

ISBN 1-872410-46-4

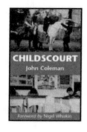

149 pages • Paperback £11.95

First published in 1967, this book is still very relevant today as it discusses the work and theories of Bill Malcolm's innovative approach to teaching and discipline in schools. Malcolm believed that democratic self-government created the best environment for learning. The school was closed recently due to Government views on Special Education.

"Interesting points that emerge are his suspicion of too much reliance on the psychiatrist and the way he has won the co-operation and admiration of the local authorities who send him pupils."
Times Literary Supplement

ENGLAND FOR THE ENGLISH

Richard Body

ISBN 1-872410-14-6

181 pages • Hardback £13.95

All three of the main political parties say they want an inclusive multi-ethnic society. But very few countries have achieved the objective without turmoil and even civil war. So how can England do it?

This book is controversial, but optimistic. England, Body argues, can have a future greater than her past.

'Sir Richard Body is the most original thinker in today's Conservative Party.'
Times Literary Supplement

'Sir Richard is a politician of unusual intelligence.'
The Daily Telegraph

FROUDE TODAY
John Coleman

ISBN 1-872410-38-3

Paperback £12.95 • Hardback £21.00

One of our great somewhat misunderstood historians whose ideas on religion, science, education and even empire that he regarded as a network of different peoples rather than a centralised organization, are as germane to today's problems as they were in Froude's own times. His research examines the motives of the most powerful players in the Europe of the sixteenth century and points to a way of understanding power in all ages.

Although this book is not about the disabled – except perhaps disabled governments – an appendix does include an interesting extract from one of Bishop von Galen's sermons preached in Munster Cathedral during the Nazi period:

Bishop von Galen does not hesitate to give concrete examples of what is happening, which he says must be opposed not by revolution but by determined resistance:

One of the patients in Marienthal [mental hospital] was a man of 55, a farmer from a country parish in the Munster region – I could give you his name – who has suffered for some years from mental disturbance and was therefore admitted to Marienthal hospital. He was not mentally ill in the full sense, he could receive visits and was always happy when his relatives came to see him. Only a fortnight ago he was visited by his wife and one of his sons, a soldier on leave from the front. The son is much attached to his father, and the parting was a sad one: no one can tell whether the soldier will return to see his father again, since he may fall in battle for his country. The son, the soldier, will certainly never again see his father on earth, for he has since then been put on the list of the 'unproductive'. A relative, who wanted to visit the father this week in Marienthal, was turned away with the information that the patient had been transferred elsewhere on the instructions of the Council of State for National Defence. No information could be given about where he had been sent, but the relatives would be informed within a few days. What information will they be given? The same as in other cases of the kind? That the man has died, that his body has been cremated, that his ashes will be handed over on the payment of a fee? The soldier risking his life in the field for his fellow-countrymen, will not see his father again on earth, because his fellow-countrymen at home have killed him.

THE CONSCIENCE OF EUROPE

Edited by John Coleman

ISBN 9-287140-30-8

212 pages • Paperback £12.00

Published by the Council of Europe in association with
New European Publications

The Council of Europe is the institution through which
the spiritual and moral leadership of Europe should be expressed. Contributors include: Cosmo Russell, Vaclav Havel, Peter Smithers and George Carey.

"The approach to the subject is decidedly spiritual, as befits an examination of conscience, and provides a welcome change from the usual economic or political analyses of the EU…"
Alain Woodrow, *The Tablet.*

"Churchmen and statesmen, poets and philosophers, each was asked to contribute a response which might be collated, with the original essay, into a compiled work. The result is truly remarkable – and in truth impossible to review."
James Bourlet, Britain and Overseas (Economic Research Council).

"The conscience of Europe is a book for both eurosceptics and europhiles. As such I recommend it highly as a means of stimulating the woefully inadequate discussion in Britain about the future of Europe."
Graham Dines, *East Anglia Daily Times.*

THE BREAKDOWN OF EUROPE
Richard Body

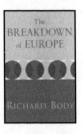

ISBN 1-872410-11-1

102 pages • Hardback £9.95

Who gains from living in a great megastate like the European Union? The moguls of international corporations find it convenient. Certain politicians enjoy the power. But for everyone else the smaller state is more prosperous, and is more congenial in every way.

Richard Body shows why the European Union will implode. Even if it survives the single currency, he explains how the electronic age will bring power back to ordinary people.

"Sir Richard Body's The Breakdown of Europe is the most thrillingly comprehensive, most sharply articulate indictment yet against the concept of deepening European integration. He speaks with the voice of truth. Every word should be heeded avidly. And acted upon; before it's too late."

Noriko Hama

"From any standpoint Richard Body has written a brilliant analysis of the most crucial issue of our time."

Lord Morris of Manchester

"To be read by everyone who believes that natural and cultural diversity is worth preserving."

Diana Schumacher